W9-AJM-655

Other Books by Father Patrick Bascio

-***The UN Was My Parish,*** Dimension Books (1979)

-***Building a Just Society,*** Orbis Books (1981)

-***The Failure of White Theology: A Black Theological Perspective,*** Peter Lang (1994)

-***Gorbachev and the Collapse of the Soviet Communist Party,*** (with co- author, Evgueny Novikov), Peter Lang. (1994)

-***A Crime of Innocence***, a novel, Dead End Street Press (2005)

-***Defeating Islamic Terrorism: The Wahhabi Factor,*** Branden Books {2007)

-***Priest to Mafia Don,*** a novel, Branden Books (2007)

-***Perfidy: The Government Cabal that Knowingly Abandoned our Prisoners of War.*** American Free Press (2008)

What They Are Saying About . . .

On the Immorality of Illegal Immigration,

By Father Patrick Bascio

"This new book, which counsels that illegal immigration is immoral, is by a devout member of a Catholic religious order in Covington, Kentucky, who takes great care to keep his tone moderate and his facts clear and accurate. He shows powerful chutzpah in confronting his church. The U.S. Conference of Catholic Bishops and numerous American cardinals seem ever anxious to open all borders and bring in any number of aliens, legal or illegal . . . Bacio understands well there are no jobs American won't do for decent wages. But the hue and cry for importing slaves has been effectively sold to Congress by businesses fronted by the U.S. Chamber of Commerce and other minority advocacy groups. The super-rich CEOs earning 400 times the average wage of their employees continue to game the system for their benefit. Bascio's book is important not because he is speaking as a Christian but because he is speaking to all Americans who believe in the rule of law and the stability of our republican government.

- Don Collins, Reviewer, *Pittsburgh Tribune*

***

"Father Bascio's book is invaluable because it furthers an internal debate over illegal immigration among Christians, especially Catholics, where there has been a stifling orthodoxy imposed by church leaders. This book develops a strong awareness of the competing moral claims from those in society who pay the substantial costs of illegal immigration. Christians rarely encounter these arguments for immigration limitation and law enforcement. His book is moving and persuasive."

- Otis L. Graham, PhD, Historian and Visiting Scholar, University of North Carolina

***

"A Christian ethicist once defined justice as 'the arithmetic of charity.' Father Bascio leaves no doubt that many Christian leaders have overlooked the injustice of illegal immigration to America's poor in their calculus of charity. Those 'leaders' earn an F the 'math of morality:' Father Bascio deserves an **A**, based on reason and scripture."

- James Edwards, PhD, Author of "A Biblical Perspective on Immigration Policy" in Carol M. Swain, ed., *Debating Immigration;* Co-Author of *The Congressional Politics of Immigration Reform*

***

"The author admits he is uncomfortable dissenting from the conventional Christian support for illegal immigration. Be he speaks out forthrightly: many vulnerable Americans, especially Black Americans, are seriously harmed by illegal immigration. Their well-being should be the first concern of American citizens."

- Albert A. Bartlett, PhD, Physicist, Boulder, CO

* * *

"Father Bascio makes a compelling case why America's poor are the chief victims of illegal immigration and why many Christian leaders fail to acknowledge its devastating impacts. Illegal immigration ensures that the most vulnerable Americans at the bottom end of the economic scale will remain there. For Father Bascio this is true social injustice that can not be tolerated."

- Leah Durant, Executive Director of Progressives for Immigration Reform, Washington, D.C; former Justice Department Attorney

* * *

"In speaking out eloquently against unfair labor competition against American workers, Father Bascio joins the proud company of Father Theodore Hesburgh, who led the 1978 Select Committee on Immigration Policy to recommend employer sanctions, and the late Father George Higgins, long-time opponent of exploitive migrant labor agreements and supporter of Caesar Chavez's resistance to the weakening of farm worker union bargaining power by illegal aliens. For those men of the cloth and, now, for Father Bascio, the real immorality of our corrupt immigration system is its victimization of America's most vulnerable citizens and legal immigrants and its defilement of the rule of law"

- Vernon Briggs, PhD, Professor of Economics, Cornell University

* * *

"Patrick Bascio, enriched by his theological formation, and years of experience with the underprivileged, offers a bold reflection on the terribly delicate issue of illegal immigration. It is bold because he tackles a question most prefer to circumvent, and because, with sound thinking and concrete examples, challenges the well-intended authorities of his own church whose perspective tends, in fact, to complicate things. He considers of the ramifications of illegal immigration that we sometimes fail to see because our perspective is insufficiently broad."

- Rev. Dominique Peridans, Assistant Pastor, St. Louis Parish, Maryland

* * *

"Father Bascio shows a special empathy for the generally ignored sufferings and abuses caused by illegal immigration and the resulting degradation in the quality of life of less fortunate Americans. Once pastor of a church in New York's Harlem, he recalls the special burden of illegal immigration on African Americans, most evident in the discrimination of local employers against black job applicants and in favor of immigrants. But the author warns that the poor are not the only victims, finding that Illegal immigration nurtures lawlessness and diminishes the security of all Americans from crime and identity fraud. The author deftly drives home his overarching argument: illegal immigration is not a victimless crime: there are an abundance of real victims, whom Christians have the moral obligation to aid and protect. A truly Christian moral approach would be, not to acquiesce in illegal immigration, but to work to end it."

- David Simcox, former Director, Center for Immigration Studies, Washington, D.C.

***

"Father Bascio has done a service to the Christian community in alerting its adherents to the fact that the most altruistic-intentioned action is fraught with unintended consequences. The chapters that resonated with me illuminated how much damage has been done to American Blacks at a time when the country was ready to open doors to employment more widely, only to have them closed again with unfair competition from illegal workers. This is to say nothing of the abuse those immigrants have suffered in low wages and dangerous conditions. Nor is it fair that the price of our charity is placed on tax-supported social services. This book would make a challenging adult-study document in the local parish."

- Rev. Robert Kyser, Retired Presbyterian Minister, Michigan

***

'It's a dangerous morality indeed that encourages the disregard of laws and borders, vital structures to our national community's peace, order and justice. The author is right on the mark when he finds that the Churches are in effect preaching that "larceny is next to godliness."

- Pete Nunez, former U.S. Attorney, San Diego; former Assistant Secretary of the Treasury for Law Enforcement.

On The Immorality of Illegal Immigration

Father Patrick J. Bascio

AuthorHouse™
1663 Liberty Drive
Bloomington, IN 47403
www.authorhouse.com
Phone: 1-800-839-8640

© 2009 Father Patrick J. Bascio. All rights reserved.

No part of this book may be reproduced, stored in a retrieval system, or transmitted by any means without the written permission of the author.

First published by AuthorHouse 9/3/2009

ISBN: 978-1-4490-0186-5 (e)
ISBN: 978-1-4490-0185-8 (sc)

Library of Congress Control Number: 2009908358

Printed in the United States of America
Bloomington, Indiana

This book is printed on acid-free paper.

Cover Photo by Martina Smiley

Chapter One

The Immorality of Illegal Immigration

It is not a pleasant task for a priest to take a position that is not shared by the hierarchy of his church. This is especially true when that hierarchy's motives stem from the gospel teachings of assisting the poor and those most adversely affected by political or economic systems. It is the function of the Christian church to make a moral judgment about economic and social matters whenever the fundamental rights of the person demand it. However, after examining all the evidence and listening to the voice of the American people, I believe that the Christian church, both here and abroad, has made a serious misjudgment, supporting a policy that has a long list of attendant evils. The Christian church currently favors an immigration policy that assists those who violate our laws rather than enter the legal process that leads to legal immigration. The Christian church, in some quarters, actually recommends to its ministers and priests that they break the law by helping illegals who break the law. The church's position disappoints those who play by the rules, placing legal immigrants and businesses that respect our laws at a great disadvantage. Americans are all completely in favor of legal immigration. That is how most Americans were lucky enough to live or be born in this great nation. Immigration is not a problem; it is, in fact, America's gift to the world. But, the simple fact is that illegal immigrants are unlawfully present in the United States and most of them are providing fraudulent documents and fraudulent identities for tax and other purposes. There are only nine digits in a Social Security number; that means that there are approximately one billion possible Social Security numbers. So, if you pick at random a nine-digit number, it is likely that you will come up with someone's valid Social Security number. The Social Security Number pool is a lottery where anyone can pick a winning number and it has no expiration date so, once an illegal alien manages to match a valid name to a valid Social Security number, it will be hard to catch him. In the meantime, he can cause untold worries and legal problems to the legitimate owner. Unfortunately, the 1986 amnesty law allowed the use of the Social Security card as proof of legal status. We need a system in which the Social Security numbers are secure.

Militancy

The year 2007 saw the rise of a militant mood among illegals south of our borders; a militant mood that insisted on the 'right' to live in the United States whether we Americans liked it or not. This is boldness never before witnessed in our history. The justification behind such militancy derived, in part, from the approbation and authority of the Christian churches. Some of them were either accompanied or led by Roman Catholic priests. I do not question the sincerity and idealism that motivated these priests. I do question their judgment. In one of those marches, in the month of March, 500,000 people took to the streets of Los Angeles, flying flags and chanting "Viva Mexico," while 500,000 marched in Dallas on April 9, using (abusing?) the image of "Our Lady of Guadalupe" on those flags. The southwestern part of the United States, they claim, as they fly the Mexican flag, belongs to them.

And what generated the anger of these crowds of illegals and their supporters? It was, believe it or not, the "temerity" of the United States to decide for the American people who could and who could not enter the United States! It did not even occur to the marchers that nowhere else in the world would they be able to mount such a bold 'invasion' without being resisted, if necessary by force. Their very lack of fear was itself an acknowledgment that the United States was the most patient and tolerant nation vis-a-vis illegal and sometimes violent entry into its territory. An invasion of twenty million people into the sovereign territory of the United States should have been responded to by demanding that the foreigners leave our soil immediately. If this demand were not met, it would be the duty of our president, in as humane a way as possible, to remove them from our territory, by force if necessary.

The Simpson-Mazzoli Act

The Mexican government became very upset with the Simpson-Mazzoli Act (Pub. L. No. 99-603, 100 Stat. 3359, signed by President Ronald Reagan on November 6, 1986). It is an Act of Congress which reformed United States immigration law. The Act made it illegal to knowingly hire or recruit undocumented workers. The Act also required employers to check on their employees' immigration status, and it granted amnesty to undocumented workers who entered the United States before January 1, 1982. Mexico was happy about the amnesty provision, but very angry with the rest. The Mexican Senate responded by adopting a strongly worded resolution on "this grave matter that negatively affects our good neighbor relations," and saying that the Act would have a negative impact on the relations between both countries. The Mexicans called it a unilateral act that should have been dealt with and decided on bilaterally, even multi-laterally. Foreseeing that this might happen, and attempting to stop such legislation, in 1984, then Mexican President Miguel de la Madrid wrote: "The situation of Mexican migrant workers in the United States has been, and continues to be, of special interest to Mexico. We have reiterated our support for the rights and interests of Mexican nationals abroad. We have no intention of meddling in the legislative processes of the United States. But we express our concern over measures such as the Simpson-Mazzoli bill which could affect the social, labor, and human rights of numerous Mexicans, whose daily work and efforts represent considerable benefit to the U.S. economy."

For a declaration that begins by saying that Mexico did not want to interfere in our affairs, the language used sure strayed along the way.

The Christian leadership of this country, not really comprehending the wide-ranging problems connected with illegal immigration has blessed violating the sovereignty of our nation, depressing the wages of American workers, encouraging the growth of the most violent gangs in America, driving up black unemployment and draining the best and brightest of the Third World, leaving it helpless. How could the church possibly desire that this state of affairs continue?

Radical Organizations

The propaganda of such rather radical organizations as The National Council of La Raza and La Voz Aztlan openly challenge America's right to protect its borders. On its Website, for example, LaVoz Aztlan also questions the legitimacy of America's major newspapers. For example, they claim the following. I quote:

1. The Wall Street Journal is read by people who run the country.
2. The New York Times is read by people who think they run the country.
3. The Washington Post is read by people who think they ought to run the country.

4. USA Today is read by people who think they ought to run the country but don't understand the Washington Post.
5. The Los Angeles Times is read by people who wouldn't mind running the country, if they could spare the time.
6. The Boston Globe is read by people whose parents used to run the country.
7. The New York Daily News is read by people who aren't too sure who's running the country.
8 The New York Post is read by people who don't care who's running the country, as long as they do something scandalous.

These organizations back the aims of a fellow-organization. Reconquista openly calls for the Reconquest of America's Mexican/U.S. border areas. A prominent sign carried by thousands at these marches and rallies tell the whole story. "If you think I'm illegal because I'm a Mexican, learn the true history because I'm in my homeland." This is not an idea that gives comfort to the average American citizen. Sometimes, La Raza gets pretty tough. In Kansas City, actions of the National Council of La Raza raised some alarm among its citizens. They threatened to boycott Kansas City and pull their national convention from the city if the mayor, Mark Funkhouser, did not remove 73-year-old Frances Semler from the Kansas City Parks Board. She came under fire from La Raza because she belonged to the Minuteman Civil Defense Corps, a neighborhood watch group that seeks to end illegal immigration by watching our southern and northern borders and reporting illegal immigration to the border patrol. Mayor Funkhouser, to his credit, stood behind Ms. Semler as long as her personal beliefs on immigration policy did not affect her service to the parks board. La Raza spokesperson, Jessica Ayala, joined five other pro-illegal immigration activists and appeared on Ms Semler's doorstep one morning. Startled by the pounding on her door and seeing the large group outside, she did what any elderly woman would do: she called police. The group responded that they were there to hand-deliver a note demanding she resign from her position on the parks board. And what is the Congress doing about all of this? When the 109th Congress (2005-2007) wrapped up its session it failed to achieve that most basic element of national sovereignty: securing America's borders. The majority of Americans made it clear that to reward ten million to twenty million individuals with the right to violate American law with impunity was immoral, just plain wrong. The American people, God bless them, saw right through the felonious nature of the bill, and knew that it penalized those who had legally applied to enter this country. They rejected it loudly and clearly, calling shame on the Congress. It was America at its best.

Thomas Jefferson

America's uniqueness derives from the belief that all men are created equal, a Jeffersonian belief that has transcended physical, psychological, and ethnic boundaries. In spite of the periodic decay imbedded in every nation-civilization, this belief has withstood the slings and arrows of outrageous misfortune for well over two hundred years. No concessions, until recently, were ever made to wholesale and flagrant violations of American sovereignty. Our recent concessions to this bold and defiant breaking of American law and the multiple evil consequences that attend it have made fools of us all, and caused us to become the butt of the international joke circuit. We have become so pitiful that even those who pour over our borders, enjoy the liberties and affluence of our wealth, are treated at our hospitals and taught in our schools, raise their native flags over the Stars and Stripes, and even, on occasion, burn our flag in the streets of our Metropolitan cities. And, meanwhile, those migrants who get lost in the maze of legal attempts to become American citizens get shortchanged, along with the businessmen who have followed the law, placing themselves, competitively, at a great disadvantage, with fellow businessmen who pay low wages to the illegals they are hiding in their business establishment. .

Alexander Hamilton

Alexander Hamilton opposed granting citizenship immediately to new immigrants: "To admit foreigners indiscriminately to the rights of citizens the moment they set foot in our country would be nothing less than to admit the Grecian horse into the citadel of our liberty and sovereignty." He recommended that when we do allow foreigners to live in America, we should make an effort "to enable aliens to ...acquire American attachments; to learn the principles and imbibe the spirit of our government; and to admit of a philosophy, at least, of their feeling a real interest in our affairs." Theodore Roosevelt wrote: "In the first place we should insist that if the immigrant who comes here in good faith becomes an American and assimilates himself to us, he shall be treated on an exact equality with everyone else, for it is an outrage to discriminate against any such man because of creed, or birth place, or origin. But this is predicated upon the man's becoming in very fact an American and nothing but an American...There can be no divided allegiance here."

Twisted and Suspect Piety

Groups that favor illegal immigration often invoke the Almighty and wrap themselves in the mantle of compassion as their justification for turning a blind eye to the terrible consequences to America of our porous borders. If simply giving somebody something they want without making them earn it is compassion, then laziness is next to godliness. The American and Mexican bishops should use their good intentions and powerful influence to remind the Mexican government that it has a responsibility for its citizens. The Mexican works for slave wages, thus impelling him to enter the United States under any conditions. Why does every discussion among American and Mexican ecclesiastics leave out the responsibility the Mexican government has for its own citizens? This is a question they must ask and answer. If it is a lack of understanding of economics and social development, then they need but acquire it from the vast academic community at their disposal. Those who preach the biblical emphasis on Sanctuary might need also to meditate on the meaning of this quote: In chapter 13 of the apostle Paul's letter to the Romans, we read: "Let every person be subject to the governing authorities. For there is no authority except from God, and those that exist have been instituted by God. Therefore, he who resists the authorities resists what God has appointed." (Romans 13:1-2).

Clearly, this is advice to Christians to follow the laws of their nation and to respect the laws of other nations. It might be better for those superiors who order their clerics to break the law by harboring illegal aliens, to use the tools available to any American and work to have the law changed. Let democracy decide this question. Although Christianity encourages acts of charity, we cannot be both charitable and law breakers. We cannot rob Peter to pay Paul. The Archbishop of Mexico City should be encouraged to work with his own backyard politicians and create a Mexico that treats its own citizens decently. He should encourage Mexicans to work for Christian social change in Mexico.

And, of course, American companies love "investing" in Third World nations.

Labor is cheap in Mexico, leaving Americans without jobs. These factories are known as "maquila." Some maquila has as many as a thousand workers. It is not unusual for some of these sweatshops to have 12-hour shifts, except on Saturdays, when the workday is nine hours. Salaries can range from thirty to fifty dollars a week. Hanes, for example, operates a t-shirt factory in Mexico. Hunger drives the local populations to work at any wage. A full-service Maquiladoras Management company based in San Diego, California, seeks American companies to "come on down."

Their Web site reads: "With a combined total of over 70 years of experience in Mexico manufacturing, the principals at Made In Mexico, Inc. are uniquely qualified to help your organization realize manufacturing cost savings." The American manufacturers cover their sins by asking us to look at the "bright side" of all this. U.S. consumers pay lower prices for clothing, and U.S. companies continue their practice of planned obsolescence, "allowing us" to replace things at a more rapid rate.

It has not occurred to a sufficient number of American workers that rather than paying a little bit less for clothing, at the expense of exploited workers around the world, the better solution, the right solution, is to pay living wages to American workers, so that they can do the jobs that "Americans will not do." The governments of Mexico and El Salvador would then be forced by internal public pressure, to pay their own workers living wages. Justice would be better served around the world if the Christian churches, armed themselves with a better understanding of the immorality of creating slave labor conditions around the world, while at the same time lowering wages in the United States for increasingly impoverished Americans.

Any elected American official who permits, encourages, or justifies illegal entry into the United States has breached his or her oath to be loyal to the Constitution. And it is inexcusable, for he or she has slept through two centuries of history as successive waves of foreigners have legally transitioned from pluribus to unum. No other nation in the world has been as generous as the United States of America in welcoming legal aliens to enter our shores and become Permanent Residents and citizens. The US averages over 1,000,000 new, legal permanent residents per year. In spite of that, illegal immigration is used by greedy business men their defenders in Congress to and with the blessing of the Christian churches, to subvert legal American wages and delay development in Third World nations. The combination of American business, their friends in Congress and the well-intentioned but immoral position of the Christian churches are leading the developed and undeveloped world to further undervelopment, affecting the lives of hundreds of millions of poor around the world. This is morally unacceptable by any standards.

The 109th Congress, with the encouragement and blessing of the Christian churches, failed to achieve that most basic governmental task of caring for its citizens and preserving normal national sovereignty. They morphed outright trickery into the proposed congressional bill of "comprehensive immigration reform." That our members of Congress, almost en masse, planned to reward many millions of illegals who had violated American laws in order to win a percentage of the illegal votes that may well be cast, is one of the low points of congressional malfeasance in American history. It is not the logic of illegal immigration that drives congressional interest in immigration; it's the desire to attract corporate contributions to their election campaigns. Everyone in Congress knows it. It is not some big, dark secret that members of Congress and the leaders of both political parties are falling all over themselves to see to it that illegal immigrants will somehow vote in the 2012 election in the hope that such law-breaking votes will usher them into the much-sought-after White House. This is an insult to all those potential immigrants who used the legal approach in their efforts to become American citizens. Every year, millions of talented and ambitious foreigners pin their hopes of a better life on getting that permission which will enable them to become Americans. They only wait for the call, and sometimes it does not come for years. They do not get the call because an illegal from their own country, who will work for lower wages, is hiding in the maze of the American factory system, being exploited. The congressional and White House plans for the American people soundly rejected comprehensive immigrant legislation, and yet the new Administration is taking another shot at it. Individual Congressmen are pandering to particular voters rather than voting for the good of the American people. To all those who are members of my church or any other American Christian church that advocate amnesty and the harboring of illegals, I say: Lets give our passion and compassion to those whose names are already sitting on waiting lists, as they hope and pray that they will have an opportunity to enter the United States legally. Any other approach is immoral. I cannot state that often enough or strongly enough. Let all of us in the Church replace emotional sympathy with an honest and educated appraisal of the multi-layered evil spawned by illegal immigration. Let us raise our collective voices and call for Mexico and other nations to get about the business of creating jobs and decent living conditions within their own borders. That is the gospel imperative.

It is Sordid

The immensely wealthy oligarchs of Latin America enjoy criticizing the plight of their fellow-Mexicans in the United States, when the very reason for the "plight" is the fact that the average Mexican farm worker earns (in pesos) the equivalent to between fifty cents and two dollars a day - and that's all day, twelve to fourteen hours. In one section of Mexico City, Netzahualcoyotl, over 1,000,000 Mexicans live in single-room "homes" that are flooded almost every time it rains. If the government of Mexico invested in producing at least some of the items American industries sell in Mexico, paid their workers decent wages, and provided them with a Bill of Rights, most Mexicans would remain at home. Amnesty disrupts Mexican family life, as the Mexican male, because of poverty, is forced to flee his home, his family and his culture. This condition benefits the wealthy oligarchy because they can leisurely continue to pay low wages to their own people. Mexican Catholic Bishops Conferences and symposiums should reflect an educated understanding of what is going on under their very noses. The captains of industry block out the cries and poverty of the poor. Only the church has the capacity to call attention to the plight of the poor. The captains of industry would rather use slave labor than compete. One irony that has escaped the notice of many is the fact that the very men who shout the loudest about maintaining a free market are the ones responsible for destroying it. It all has to do with smoke and mirrors and a terrible dishonesty. These Mexican captains of industry work overtime to see to it that the money pool created by cheap labor never ends for them. That is precisely why Jesus said: "It is more difficult for a camel to pass through the eye of a needle than for a rich man to enter the Kingdom of Heaven". Mexican investments in their people are the key. For our part, there is no shortage of American workers to take jobs in restaurants, produce farms, granaries, construction sites or meat-packing plants.

Our Congress should divert its attention from the next electoral cycle and look at the long-term economic consequences to the American workingman of a very cheap, Latin American illegal labor force that is willing to work without Workers Comp insurance and below standard-of-living wages. And let the liberal politicians who cry "Justice for the

Poor" in the marketplace while promoting "comprehensive immigration legislation" know of the harm they are doing to both the Mexican and American economies. Politics makes strange bedfellows, but the alliance of conservatives, liberals and corporate interests is one of the most insidious and outstanding examples of being corrupted by big money. The spin put on hiring illegals is the idea that American corporations will go under unless they exploit illegal workers. That is ridiculous, and no one knows this better than the business community.

Along the border, state police frustrated at the lack of government support and action, have been acting more aggressively to enforce the law. The Irving, California police department has been working to identify illegal immigrants who have been arrested, and deport them. Since the program began (as of the fall of 2007) Irving police have turned over more than more than 2000 illegals to immigration officials. The campaign to round up illegal aliens has seen a tenfold increase in deportations. Federal officers in Southern California in late October 2007 arrested more than 1,300 immigrants, most of whom either had criminal records or had failed to abide by deportation orders. Having been rebuffed in an attempt to declare the equivalent of amnesty, the Bush administration began to use a new strategy. The strategy was is to crack down more severely on illegal aliens in the hope that in doing so the president would get one more shot at passing his immigration bill before he left office. That did not happen.

Even in Antwerp

The immorality of supporting illegal immigration is not an issue confined to the United States. In Antwerp's leading Catholic newspaper, (May, 2006) *Gazet van Antwerpen*y , Prof. Robert Senelle, one of Belgium's leading constitutionalists, states that Prime Minister Guy Verhofstadt was obliged to call the Papal Nuncio to account because "church asylum" is a violation of article 268 of the Belgian Penal Code which forbids priests to put pressure on the government in order to have the law altered. "Belgium simply cannot regularize 40,000 illegals without papers. This wild immigration will be a disaster for the country," Senelle wrote. What began as a desire to implement the beautiful social teaching of the Gospel ended in chaos. Many Catholics complained about the desecration of Belgian churches by men and women "sharing beds in church, lighting fires and cooking on the floors, installing radios and televisions, removing altars and tabernacles, covering images of saints and displaying banners with the name of Allah." In Saudi Arabia, such an action performed by Christians would result in the death sentence.

Marco Laenens, an Antwerp politician for the governing Liberal Party, accused Catholic Church groups of subverting the government and nation. Monsignor Karl-Jozef Rauber, the Papal Nuncio to Belgium, who had earlier strongly supported the illegal immigration movement, changed his mind after evoking critical government reaction. The Nuncio's secretariat denied that Monsignor Rauber supported the illegals' actions, saying: "The Nuncio cannot interfere in this issue. However, whatever the Belgian bishops say, the Nuncio supports them because the bishops, he says, are wise men." I agree with the age-old Catholic theological dictum: *Sensus Populi, Sensus Ecclesiae,* i.e. the mind of the people should be reflected in the mind of the church. And Christians everywhere agree that no one has nationally-proclaimed rights unless he or she is a citizen of that nation. Neither church nor state should give even the slightest impression that the illegal immigrant is not obliged to obey the laws of the host nation. If the laws of the country were truly respected, the illegal immigrant would not be there in the first place. Giving amnesty to those breaking the law would be like the police telling a robber, after he has been apprehended: "You can go now, but from now on try and obey the law."

Aiding and Abetting Impoverishment

Economists have recognized the negative consequence of the brain drain to the Third World for decades. It leaves those nations, already physically impoverished, intellectually and innovatively impoverished. By accepting local underdevelopment as the price of amnesty, those who wish the Third World worker well are doing exactly the opposite. Everyone loses except the business and political establishments. It is true that adding foreign doctors indiscriminately may be able to drive down American doctors' wages over time, but so would expanding the number of American medical students allowed to enter

American medical schools. If the AMA can accept the lowering of wages for American doctors by importing cheap labor doctors from around the world, they can accept the lowering of wages by filling up our medical schools with young American men and women who try every year to get in, but are turned away. There is plenty of space. Those who build their empires by constructing the world economic order on the foundation of cheap labor are immoral and their sins cry out to heaven for vengeance. Church leaders, we plead with you to take note of this. If anything is crystal clear in the gospel it is to rescue the poor and disadvantaged from their miserable living conditions.

Bank of America

American banks openly court illegal alien business and give them home mortgage loans in violation of federal law. For Bank of America, the policy is good business. Under the tenure of Attorney General Gonzalez there was little or no indictment of these banks. The Wall Street Journal reported that, as of February 2006, Bank of America began offering credit cards in Los Angeles to people without a Social Security numbers or credit histories. This it did so long as they had held a checking account with the bank for three months with no overdrafts. The bank has since expanded the program. This did not sit well with Americans. An America Online poll with over 47,000 people voting shows that 86% disapprove of Bank of America's decision to give credit cards to illegals! *Business Journal* readers gave their opinion. In an online survey, 81 percent of 457 respondents think Bank of America is encouraging illegal immigration and should stop. Public demonstrations against the bank have taken place. One such demonstration took place in front of the White House on April 22, 2007.

Americans Angry

What we're beginning to see is an uprising of American citizens who have been awakened to the stark reality of what illegal immigration is doing to this country, and what an enormous burden it is placing on the taxpayer. If it could be shown that all this sacrifice and dislocation actually assisted the Third World in closing the economic and technological gap between the rich and the poor, then Americans might decide that they would voluntarily accept the general lowering of human and financial standards that come with illegal immigration. However, the opposite is the case. Since the biggest moral force in America and around the world in encouraging illegal immigration is the church, it behooves churchmen to become knowledgeable in the dire consequences of that which they are supporting in the name of the gospel. As we begin to close in on the issue and demand that our legislators enforce the laws, illegal aliens are even more desperately seeking protection from the church. The primary obligation of the church, precisely because it is key to solving the problem of the imbalance between the First and the Third World, is to embark on a major intellectual and moral study of the issues involved. It needs to recognize that a new policy based on Third World development is the only long-term solution. When this problem is solved there will be no excuse for illegal immigration. It would give an opportunity for hundreds of millions of poverty-stricken people to earn a decent living at home without the need for disrupting family and conjugal life. It would also bring to an end the necessity of illegals hiding from the law in developed nations and sparing their children the traumatic effects of suddenly having to grow up in a foreign culture and surroundings, far from friends and family.

In his famous commentary on the United States, *American Democracy*, Alex De Tocqueville said that what he observed going on in America was that American religious leaders had a deeper understanding of democracy than that which he found among his fellow Europeans. Americans, he wrote, gave more weight to simple common sense and reason in their lives as religious people. And this phenomenon, he observed, was very important in the formation of democracy. He thought that the American way of practicing religion paid more attention to the human mind than was the case in Europe, There, he said, the approach to religion either wallowed in sentimentalism or arrogantly dismissed it. The American style of restraining emotion, and paying more attention to reason than sentimentalism, produced the most religious nation in the world. The vast majority of Christians in our nation strongly oppose the church leadership with respect to having a hiring hall on church property where employers have access to illegals that they exploit with low wages and no benefits. It strikes a sour note in workingmen and women. The church needs to look beyond the rose-colored glasses of "compassion for the poor" and assess the worldwide consequences of continuing to support a way of life that is devastating the Third World, and causing confusion, dislocation and the lowering of living standards at home. One letter to the editor written by a subscriber to a San Diego newspaper made a good point. "Any church that supports illegals should have to pay taxes to help communities that have to provide education and health benefits to illegals. It is time that churches that disobey laws pay for it and lose their tax exempt status."

Chapter Two

The Illegal Immigrant Component of America's Street Gangs

In 2005 alone more than two hundred vehicles stolen in Arizona were shipped overseas for sale. Others were stolen and are either being used in Arizona or shipped to other States. A large number of them service some of the 500,000 illegals living in Arizona. At a conservative average of $15,000 per vehicle, owner losses exceeded one billion dollars. Insurance companies are reeling at the enormous claims coming from policyholders. Beyond Arizona, thousands of illegals kill, rob, rape, and molest Americans who live near or in our inner cities. Although illegals constitute only 4 percent of our population, they represent 28 per cent of our convicts. They are infesting and causing untold suffering in a multitude of America's major cities. According to Article IV, Section 4 of the U. S. Constitution, "The United States shall guarantee to every State in this Union a

Republican Form of Government, and shall protect each of them...against domestic Violence." To put it simply, although our government is obliged to keep us safe from any enemy, foreign or domestic, it is not doing so. Both the president and the Christian leadership in America, in working to legalize illegal aliens, are aiding and abetting the most dramatic and dangerous proliferation of violence that our nation's cities have ever known. That is simply outright immoral. According to *Newsweek,* March 28, 2005, over 10,000 MS-13 gang members illegally crossed our borders looking for a way to enrich themselves. They are backed by 40,000 in Central Americas. The MS-13 members are identified by numerous tattoos splashed all over their bodies and faces, and the wearing of the blue and white colors taken from the El Salvadoran flag. An article, *'The Most Dangerous Gang in America'* profiles how criminal illegal aliens cross our borders to loot and murder, making the lives of millions of Americans a virtual nightmare. MS-13 members can be as young as twelve years of age. They have become Central America's greatest problem and the gang has moved into the United States big time. In Central America it has carried out violent acts against the government. In 1997, the son of Honduran president Ricardo Maduro was kidnapped and murdered by MS-13 members. They also sent a message to the Honduran president, pinning a note to a dismembered corpse that read "more people will die... the next victims will be police and journalists." In 2004, Guatemalan President

Oscar Berger received an identical message. Whatever family values exist for illegal immigrants in their home countries, for some they certainly stop at the Rio Grande. In fact, since 1999, there have been more than 1,000,000 sex crimes committed in the United States by illegal aliens. The next time someone tells you that illegal immigration is a "victimless crime," remind them of the raped whose lives will never be the same!

Michelle Malkin, an author on illegal immigration, was interviewed in October, 2002. An excerpt from her book reported one of many very brutal murders and rapes committed by Angel Resendez in his killing sprees. He has been called the Angel of death. "On Friday, April 30, 1999, the Reverend Norman "Skip" Sirnic and his wife Karen went to bed and looked forward to the weekend`s busy church activities. That Sunday was the Reverend Sirnic`s birthday. Their red pickup truck was parked outside the parsonage, located about fifty yards from the Southern Pacific train tracks that crossed the town. Resendez broke into the rear of the couple's home as they slept and grabbed a twelve-pound sledgehammer from a garage closet. He struck the Reverend Sirnic twice as he slept, killing him instantly. His wife sustained a vicious blow to the face and was raped. I don't need to go on."

The list is endless. Are Mexican young men, by their nature, less moral than American young men? Not at all; but their lives of less-than-human economic conditions twist their psyches and they find a way to act out their desperation at the poverty in which they live. Now they act out their frustrations and anger in America's ghettos. There is the Eighteenth Street Gang with twenty thousand mostly illegal alien members in Los Angeles, the Chinese Mafia in New York, Hispanic Bloods and Crips in Los Angeles, and a growing gang cartel from El Salvador. I have never heard, even once, in a major speech to the American people, our president address this great and criminal danger to American citizens. Let me remind you that he has an obligation under Article IV, section 4 of the Constitution, to protect America. Am I surprised he has not made a major speech on such an important subject? Not really. I recently published a book on Islamic terrorism, pointing out that neither President Bush, nor Condoleeza Rice, nor Vice President Cheney, nor the Republican or Democratic Party leaders have ever mentioned the source of Islamic terrorism. Not one of them came to a microphone and stated in straight, unvarnished language that the religious establishment of Saudi Arabia, the Wahhabi, funds Islamic terrorism. Heavily funded by the Saudi government, they established Osama bin Laden and his al Qaeda network, and continue to be the primary financial support of Islamic terrorism. Not a word about it to us from our government. Amazing. So, both on the international scene with the Wahhabi, and on the national scene with the growing number of very brutal and criminal gangs heavily composed of illegal immigrants, is it not fair to ask the question: Is our government protecting us? In my home state of Massachusetts, two MS-13 members raped two teenage girls. Others of the gang hacked four fingers of a sixteen year old with machetes. These men not only have been trained in the deadly use of the machete as a weapon of choice, but many of them were members of the highly trained El Salvador military. President Bush, President Obama and the Congress know of their existence, but no alarms and no attempt at public support for a determined move against these dangers has ever become a publicly-declared goal either of the White House or the Congress. It does appear that in the rarified atmosphere of Washington, the oxygen of truth evaporates.

Our Government Dysfunctional?

At their request, I have also studied the problems suffered by the POW/MIA community in the United States. The members of that community, spread from Maine to California, have been frustrated since 1973 in their attempts to discover if their missing POW/MIA sons, fathers and husbands are still alive in Southeast Asia. They are terribly and painfully suffering because of our government's unwillingness to discover or share the truth of their location in Vietnam, Cambodia and Laos. Has our government, a government comprised, in the main, of decent citizens, become dysfunctional? Has the Christian leadership in our nation confined the scope of its religious enquiry to the exciting but relatively insignificant details of liturgical practice? Where are the Christian prophetic role models? Are we now going through the same process of trying but failing to get the Government to act to preserve our cities from mayhem and murder? Would not ten thousand armed and deadly men who have crossed our borders illegally be considered enemy combatants? Bob Clifford, who directs the FBI unit to track MS-13, describes the group as having developed from a collection of loosely organized cells across America, to an increasingly dangerous organization, a threat to public safety. Please, President Obama, protect us; change your position on immigration policy. If you do, you will leave office with the gratitude of millions of your fellow-Americans, especially those who live in our inner cities. You will challenge the Mexican and other governments to treat their own citizens decently. Americans are crying out that neither the church nor the government should be complicit in the invasion of illegal immigrants who make up the most murderous and lethal gangs in the history of this nation. With over 500,000 illegal aliens in our prisons and at least one million more pouring into our nation annually, competency and alertness on the part of both church and state is essential to America's future.

MS-13

MS-13, alias La Mara Salvatrucha, specializes in horrific crime scenes, brutally hatcheting, murdering and torturing Americans, from children to teenagers and adults. They act indiscriminately for the thrill of it and apparently, in most cases, without a specific motive except, perhaps, the thrill of it. Mara is the Spanish word for "army ant", and "Salvatrucha," the slang for "Salvadoran". The MS-13 originated in Los Angeles. The gang was set up in 1972 by Salvadoran immigrants. Initially, it allowed only Salvadorans to join, but later allowed, first, any Hispanics and then other nationalities. The Mara Salvatrucha gangs have cliques, or factions located throughout the United States and Latin America. Membership is believed to total over 100,000 worldwide. Some gang members from the Los Angeles area have been deported because of their illegal status in the United States, but since the rules for deporting illegal immigrants are not currently in favor in Washington, implementation is haphazard at best, and criminal replacements come across our borders in a steady stream. Those who are deported back to Central America either join gangs already in place at home, start gangs of their own, or simply stroll back across the US border. In 2005, Chicago Police Superintendent Philip J. Cline compared Mafia and MS-13 violence. He said that MS-13 is much more violent than the Italian Mafia, explaining that while the Mafia killed 1,111 people since 1919, MS-13 and their criminal friends have killed 1,276 people just since 2000. We desperately need the same Christian church that supported amnesty in the 2007 debate on Capitol Hill, to reverse its position and fight against it. The moral authority of the Christian church is needed to support the tightening of our borders and the deportation of criminal illegal immigrants. At the moment, there appears to be no likelihood of that, but I will continue to hope.

MS-13, composed primarily of Catholics, is the fastest growing and most violent of America's street gangs, so fearsome that other gangs, equally violent, fear them. They have left their mark from El Salvador to Honduras to Guatemala to New Mexico, as well as thirty-three American states, with northern Virginia, southern Maryland and the Washington, D.C. area now being heavily infiltrated. Their biggest concentrations are in Long Island, New York and California, their birthplace. They divide their manpower according to the parts of our nation most vulnerable to the drug trade. Not a group willing to put up with opposition, according to the U.S. Department of Homeland Security, it sent out a memo warning border patrol agents that they could now become targets of assassination if they attempt to take their jobs seriously. The memo complained that border patrols were having a negative effect on their smuggling business. How can the United States possibly recruit young men and women to sign up for the United States Border Patrol if the illegal immigrants are able to intimidate American law enforcement so brazenly? The bad guys are more heavily armed with sophisticated weapons than the border agents. The Border Patrol agents are between a rock and a hard place. If they do not open fire quickly enough they may lose their lives or that of their partners. If they do open fire quickly they may be prosecuted, losing the ability to defend us and support their own families. MS-13 uses violence to their advantage to make sure that whatever message they're sending out is heard by everyone. One Miami investigative officer spearheading that police department's investigation into MS-13 opened his door one day to discover a bullet with his name on it on the doorstep. We are running out of time to save our cities from massive dislocation and suffering. These are not just my words; they are the words of all the major law enforcement agencies of our nation. The major institution, the Christian church, by its influence and its reputation for being the conscience of this great nation, needs to reverse direction, come up to the plate and hit a home run for the good of the American people. It needs to put its focus on welcoming and assisting legal immigrants. This is what made this nation the shining beacon of hope it has become worldwide. With the help of the Christian Church it can continue to be just that.

The Eighteenth Street Gang

Assuming we conclude that MS-13 is the most vicious street gang in America, the Eighteenth Street Gang in Los Angeles ranks second in ferocity and is much larger. Law enforcement officers have estimated that there are thirty thousand Eighteenth Street gang members, of thirty different subsets, in California alone. Its membership consists primarily of Mexicans and Chicanos with some Salvadorans and a smattering of blacks. They usually group together in smaller units to form a faction, each faction having fifty to several hundred members each. Factions of the Eighteenth Street Gang are dispersed primarily throughout San Fernando Valley, San Gabriel Valley, South Bay, and South Los Angeles.

Ethnic Cleansing

Another development taking place is that the Eighteenth Street Gang and MS-13 gang have declared ethnic cleansing zones in Los Angeles. In these zones of the city, blacks cannot enter without fear of assassination. Brown-on-black violence is becoming routine, regardless of gang affiliation. The violence takes place in our prisons, our schools, and on the streets. Illegal immigrants, fresh from crossing our borders, and members of Central American gangs, have openly and without fear of punishment declared a policy of ethnic cleansing against black Americans. You ask, is that possible? Yes, it's a fact. Obviously these illegal immigrants have very high ambitions and feel so secure from legal authorities in America that, although they may have been in America for only a few weeks, they are openly murdering black and white Americans. One such victim was Nickson Gilles, a young black man from Canoga Park Florida, a talented football athlete and student at Pierce College. His ambition was to do well enough at Pierce to earn him a transfer over to USC and then, if lucky, to play in the NFL. It never happened. It is alleged that a member of the Latino Canoga Park Alabama gang killed him with a shotgun blast after his first football game of the season. The Latino gang is proud of its policy of targeting African-Americas in America. Ironically, two year prior to this incident, Canoga Park won the prestigious All-America City designation because of its racial harmony in the midst of ethnic diversity. Illegal immigrant gangsters had struck once again. .

Progress

So, is anyone doing anything? Yes, on a small scale. Los Angeles now has thirty-three permanent injunctions involving fifty gangs, and that has produced some results. The injunctions prohibit gang members, RICO-statute style, from associating with each other, carrying weapons, possessing drugs, committing crimes and displaying gang symbols in a safety zone. This also bans them from possessing alcohol in public areas even if they're of age. A violation of this order results in a misdemeanor charge and up to a year in jail. Prosecutors say the possibility of jail stays is a strong deterrent. Violent crime has dropped 13 percent in the Wichita Falls area of Texas, as a result of injunctions. However, some commentators on the issue say that the injunctions are on particular areas, so when they are issued the gang members simply move to another area. Shades of Iraq? So, perhaps, the 13 per cent drop is not all that significant.

White House Leadership Needed

In 2004, the FBI created the MS-13 National Gang Task Force, but what is needed is leadership right out of the White House, because this is an ongoing national emergency. At an International conference held on gang enforcement in San Salvador it was said that the ultra violent MS-13 gangs are now present in 3,500 U.S. cities. In the opening session, El Salvadoran president Antonio Saca said the problem is one that should concern many nations. He said, "Gangs like MS-13 have evolved into coordinated and well-financed criminal organizations," making them an international problem. And yet, in the FBI's D.C. field office, after 9/11, the number of agents dedicated to gang investigations has declined by 50 percent. There was a definite shift in resources post-9/11 toward foreign terrorism. But sadly, during this same period of time, our local terrorists, the Eighteenth Street and MS-13 gangs have moved on to a higher degree of sophistication and organization, as they develop closer ties with the Mexican and Colombian drug cartels.

New Jersey Acts

One law enforcement agency got stirred into action in August of 2007 at the execution-style killings of three Newark college students and the wounding of a fourth victim. The state attorney general ordered New Jersey law enforcers to notify federal immigration officials whenever someone arrested for an indictable offense or drunken driving is found to be an illegal immigrant. Attorney General Anne Milgram reviewed the state's policy in light of the fact that one of the six suspects was an illegal immigrant who had been granted bail on child rape and aggravated assault charges without immigration officials being alerted to his existence. Ms. Milgram said that if the policy had been in place when Jose Carranza was indicted on the prior charges, federal officials might have placed an immigration hold on him. He would have been off the streets. Ms Milgram admitted that prior to her issuing of this directive "all police departments in our state had complete discretion as to if, when and how to notify immigration authorities." The illusionary and immoral act of sanctuary for those who break the law was bound to end badly. If the Founding Fathers were meeting in Philadelphia today, we would hear them shouting. "We fixed this problem three hundred years ago. Looks like we need to fix it again."

As I close this chapter, let me quote a shortened version of the testimony given by Heather MacDonald, a senior fellow at the Manhattan Institute for Policy Research, a think tank in New York City. Ms.MacDonald has analyzed illegal immigration for the City Journal and the Los Angeles Times, among other publications.

> "Sanctuary laws are a serious impediment to stemming gang violence and other crime. Sanctuary laws, present in such cities as Los Angeles, New York, Chicago, Austin, Houston, and San Francisco, generally forbid local police officers from inquiring into a suspect's immigration status or reporting it to federal authorities. Such laws place a higher priority on protecting illegal aliens from deportation than on protecting legal immigrants and citizens from assault, rape, arson, and other crimes. Under the prevailing understanding of Los Angeles's sanctuary law (special order 40), if (an) officer merely inquires into the gangbanger's immigration status he will face departmental punishment.
>
> "To get the felon off the street, the cop has to

wait until he has probable cause to arrest the gangbanger for a non-immigration crime, such as murder or robbery. A confidential California Department of Justice study reported in 1995 that 60 percent of the 20,000-strong Eighteenth Street Gang in southern California is illegal; police officers say the proportion is actually much greater.

--Law enforcement officials estimate that 20% of gang members in San Diego County are illegal, according to the Union-Tribune.

--The leadership of the Columbia Lil' Cycos gang was about 60 percent illegal in 2002. Francisco Martinez, a Mexican Mafia member and an illegal alien, controlled the gang from prison...

--In Los Angeles, 95 percent of all outstanding warrants for homicide in the first half of 2004 (which totaled 1,200 to 1,500) targeted illegal aliens.

--The Los Angeles Police Department arrests about 2500 criminally-convicted deportees annually, reports the Los Angeles Times.

"The standard argument for sanctuary laws is that they encourage illegal aliens to work with the police or seek government services. This argument is based on myth, not evidence. No illegal alien advocate has ever provided a shred of evidence that sanctuary laws actually accomplish their alleged ends. The idea that sanctuary laws are "pro-immigrant" is perhaps the greatest myth of all."

Thank you, Heather McDonald. Your eloquent testimony certainly makes the case that to support sanctuary laws and support amnesty for illegal aliens is immoral. The church and state need to reflect on this fact. There are enough legal immigrants in this nation who need assistance to keep the Christian church very busy exercising its mandate to assist the poor and continue to build up the Kingdom of God in this our native land.

Chapter Three

The Brain Drain: Immoral Legal Immigration

The Christian church, in its noble efforts to assist the world's poor, is desperately in need of economic expertise and must dig into its own wonderful theological journey of the last two thousand years to learn and articulate for the Christian community a clearer understanding of what constitutes human dignity. Part of that understanding should be the meaning and the cause of 'the brain drain.' Economics 101 introduced a multitude of students to that expression and the extent to which the brain drain has further underdeveloped already underdeveloped nations around the world. The phrase "brain drain" was coined in the 1960s when the United States began to hoard UK doctors. In that case, one developed country, the US, dispossessed another (the UK). The US, emerged from the Second World War in 1944 with 80 percent of the world's gold reserve in bullions, the other, the UK, had been severely hit and deprived of its empire in the course of the war. To lose many of their most brilliant medical personnel was a further blow both to their self-esteem and to the option of producing medical miracles in their own nation. Shimon Peres, ninth president of Israel, eighth prime minister of Israel (three times), finance minister, foreign minister, and defense minister had these words of wisdom for all of us: "Now that the (world's) land is generally distributed, a new type of war has appeared. the war about technology and its control. This is, I believe, the new threat for the upcoming century "

We Need the Jesuits

Included in the concept of 'brain drain' is 'entrepreneurship', i.e. the innovative gift that a nation's talented citizens contribute to its economic well-being and development. One of the main engines of entrepreneurship is a well-developed university system that brings on board the brightest minds of a nation. Without such a system no amount of rhetoric and no amount of effort spent on amnesty for illegal immigrants will be in the best interests of the poor. If the church mobilized its resources to 'hire' the Jesuit community to found and develop great universities in Central America, then what talent left in Central America can be channeled to local development and local appreciation of the particular charism and character God implanted in Central America. If the Christian church wishes to really help Central America and Mexico, then it can also call on the international corporations to share a given amount of their technological expertise to that part of the world, so that local high tech companies can be formed. The young Third World scientists graduating from Jesuit universities can man these companies. The Jesuit universities could, as is the custom all over the world, assign these students to temporary programs offered in the developed world, to get some hands-on experience for as long as it takes to complete a particular study or project. Also, new internet and podcast tools are constantly being developed and improved that would enable less time spent abroad than in prior similar programs.

Hope in Zimbabwe

The Church could look at the initiative that one man in Zimbabwe took when that nation had to face the loss of Zimbabwe's healthcare and many other professionals to industrialized nations. According to a Scientific and Industrial Research and Development Centre (SIRDC) study, more than 500 000 Zimbabweans, many of them professionals, have left the country because of poor salaries, working conditions and dim prospects for job advancement. Zimbabwean professor Chetsanga sees no hope for the future of young Zimbaweans unless the government provids the necessary industrial base to retain professionals. Chetsanga said: "It is an economic factor. It is no longer political; it is strictly economic. Our industrial sector is down; the economic performance is down. For the economy to retain skilled professionals our industry has to be alive and kicking and our agricultural sector too, has to be alive and kicking." A performing industry and agriculture sector, he says, is critical for the country's economic recovery as well as the retention of skilled professionals. "We don't seem to be on a recovery path; we are sliding downwards," says Prof Chetsanga who is the inaugural president of the Zimbabwe Academy of Sciences, a body made up of the country's intelligentsia. But not all hope is lost. The renowned biochemist says the Government must expand the higher education system to mitigate the effects of brain drain. "By expanding our higher education system, we are expanding our feeder lines. We have more than half a million students in universities and in theory we should be graduating half a million students every year." Chetsanga said that which is so obvious: Britain, Australia and the United States are the biggest magnets of doctors, nurses and other health practitioners from Zimbabwe. In 2003 alone, a total of 2825 work permits were granted to doctors and nurses from Zimbabwe in the United Kingdom while 5880 work permits were issued to health professionals from South Africa.

The government, aided by the international community which itself needs to be prodded by church and state, must focus on networking with professionals in the diaspora, investing more in research and improving working conditions. Zimbabwe has thirteen universities and if more resources were invested in human development — training of more doctors, nurses, dentists and other health professionals--- the country would eventually reach a point of equilibrium, retaining enough healthcare staff while at the same time exporting to gain from migrant labor remittances. Nearly one in ten tertiary-educated adults (those with some university or post-secondary schooling) born in the developing world — between a third and half of the developing world's science and technology personnel — now live in the developed world. Since these immigrants (legal or illegal) with skills are desperately needed at home, the church should encourage them to remain at home, by offering an alternative to the practice of many Third World leaders. Third World leaders are far more interested in encouraging the immediate monetary results of encouraging their best brains to cross our borders. The World Bank's Global Economic Prospects 2006 report estimated total remittances of $232 billion in 2005, including $167 billion received by developing countries, almost double the $86 billion in 2000. This is money that comes in freely, without any work being done in the nation of origin to develop national industry. It is a deal the Third World leaders are unable to refuse. They can just sit back, let their nation go to pot, and watch the money pour in from the United States, most of which ends up in the pockets of the greedy and well-placed elite. Of course, we can all rejoice at the relief the families of these immigrants receive from such remittances. We should not begrudge them that. But, the point is that all of this puts the day of development that much further into the future. It is immoral, and the church should say so.

Extent of Brain Drain

How extensive is the "brain drain?" There are tried and trusted principles of economics that have dealt with this question extensively. As a generality, there is the common sense principle that the more highly educated a person is, the better opportunity does he or she have to earn a living wage or better. Of course, let me quickly add that the brain drain, whether legal or illegal, can only be solved if the highly educated person, if he or she is from a Third World nation, remains there and contributes to the local economy. So, in principle, it is immoral for church or state to recommend amnesty to illegal immigrants because, especially at the wages they receive, these laborers add to corporation profits and do not assist in any way development in their own nation. All the developed world's efforts to increase aid to the Third World are negated in practical terms because the competent personnel able to implement aid efforts have fled to Europe and the United States. Among the countries in Asia and the Pacific, the biggest source is the Philippines, with 730,000 migrants. While Philippine health services are deplorable, there is scarcely a major city in the United States whose hospitals are not graced with the wonderful service Philippine nurses contribute to our health services. There are now 750,000 Philippine migrants who cannot contribute directly to developing an economic and social infrastructure to make the Philippines a safe and decent place in which to live, bear children and enjoy their old age among family, friends and a culture that is their own.

Every year there are 20,000 fewer highly qualified persons in Africa who can manage key public services, develop economic growth, and call for greater democracy. The migration of Africans with only a primary education is almost nil. Chinese migrants to the United States number 400,000, split almost equally between the secondary and tertiary educational groups. Both India and Korea have each seen well over 300,000 people migrate to the United States since 1990. It is striking that more than 75 percent of Indian immigrants have a tertiary education. The brain drain to the United States from many Central American and Caribbean countries is substantial: 42 percent for Jamaica and 46 percent for Trinidad and Tobago. More than seventy percent of Guyanese immigrants to the United States have a tertiary education; fifty three percent of Korean immigrants have a tertiary education. The biggest migratory flows from Africa to the United States are from Egypt, Ghana, and South Africa, with more than 60 percent of immigrants from those three countries having a tertiary education. There are two reasons for them to be incorporated into a plan to developing their own nations, but they will take the job that their American counterpart could have. The United States corporate community is hurting two entities at the same time: Third World development and the U.S. middle class. This is immoral.

Europe As Well

The brain drain to the United States is also a phenomenon of Western Europe, but the educational opportunities provide relatively easy replacement. Nevertheless, a few years ago E.U. leaders, with this brain drain in mind, bravely made a decision to make the European Union "the most competitive and dynamic knowledge-based economy in the world" by 2010. Well, at this writing we are well into 2009 and that particular dream shows serious signs of non-fulfillment because immigrants like Albert Einstein and Enrico Fermi continue to sail or fly from Europe to the United States in a constant stream. One half million of Europe's best and brightest scientific brains pursue careers in the U.S. One half million!!! If two and two is four, then one half million is brain drain of a serious nature.

Watching all of this happening from the sidelines prompted Britain's Royal Society to coin the expression "brain drain", as they saw some of their best scientists leave important work for human development and flock to the United States. The billions of dollars that were being spent on the arms race attracted them. The church was not as silent then. It did address the issue, but took into account the political and religious persecution that caused some of it. Even the university establishment has been somewhat understanding, pointing to the heavily bureaucratic rules and regulations that can sometimes smother genius and entrepreneurship in Europe.

The church should mount its collective pulpit, put on its prophetic cloak and shout at the top of its lungs, "Enough. Enough. Stop greedily running after money. Stay home and see to your brothers and sisters, your mothers and fathers, your religious, intellectual, cultural and economic heritage." Its failure to do so bespeaks an impoverished intellectual understanding of what constitutes immorality. The duty of the Christian church is to offer alternatives that will not penalize poor nations further by draining them of their best minds and their poorest masses. In the Catholic church there is an abundance of priests very capable of setting up a think tank to examine the problem and come up with solutions. If the biblical truism that to whom much has been given much will be demanded were to be applied to the Catholic church today, then the well-meaning should rally the Jesuits, the Dominicans and other religious orders and congregations to think-tank this problem through. The congressional and White House comprehensive proposal is the byproduct of the insatiable greed of international corporations and the illusion on the part of politicians that by supporting this so-called comprehensive proposal they will win votes in the next election. It is illusory not in the sense that the garnering of votes would not happen; it is illusionary in the sense that earthly power itself is illusory. Very few men have been as frequently quoted as Lord Acton. Power corrupts and absolute power corrupts absolutely.

European Brain Drain

Let's take a look at the European brain drain to the United States. One would have to be a linguist to have a conversation with the staffs of many research facilities spread right across this nation. What attracts them? Money. The salary an Italian, French or German scientist/researcher can make in New York,

Chicago, or San Francisco is three times that which he or she would receive at home. It is as simple as that. Could they make a good living at home? Yes, of course, but good compared to excellent does not stand a chance. However, it is not only money that tempts European scientists to flee to the United States. It's also the European bureaucracy. European scientists and researchers complain of the rigid control exercised on them and their work, and the poor salaries. Some researchers have earned as low as 6 euros an hour. They envy the relatively free academic atmosphere of the American university and research center. Nor does their Church encourage them to stay at home for the sake of their nation, their culture, the nation's academic excellence. But there is some hope for the future. The Europeans know that not one of them, singly, can match the economic powerhouse that is America. They realize that if that situation continues, Europe may not become a Third World nation but it could, collectively, become a Second World nation. So, they hope to develop a European research area for pooling expertise in an effort to a least stand their ground, even if they are unable to challenge the mighty American position at the top of the hill. If Europe has any hope of continuing its universal health care system, it needs to make more economic progress.

Canada

Between 1960 and 1990, the United States and Canada received more than one million professional immigrants and experts from Third World countries. They are a collective sponge that absorbs the best and brightest of the world's talent, devastating the chances of a better future for the nations they abandon. In the health care sector,

Canada has experienced a southward exodus by physicians and nurses to the US, causing health care cuts in Canada. Not surprising. The American Competitiveness in the 21st Century Act —approved by the US Congress in 2000— upped the temporary work visa (H-1B) allotment, from 65 thousand to 115 thousand in the 2000 fiscal year and then to 195 thousand for fiscal years 2001 through 2003. The aim of this increase was to tempt highly qualified immigrants to the United States. Canada is in trouble. The CD Howe Institute reported that the brain drain to the US is "real and costly." It produced tables indicating that since the 1980s the loss of professionals had jumped by 54 per cent, the loss of managers by 78 per cent. More recently, the Conference Board of Canada claimed that the number of Canadians applying for temporary work permits in the US increased more than fivefold. Swiss Business School, IMD, published a yearbook in which Canada was ranked tenth among forty-seven countries when it came to competitiveness, but only thirty- sixth in terms of its ability to retain well-educated people. On the health care front, the loss of a single physician can be devastating. The loss of an anesthetist can set off a series of negatives, ending in the termination of scheduled surgery and patients sent home. The Canadian Institute for Health Information has reported a shortfall of 180 anesthetists across the country. They are probably sipping iced tea in Palm Beach, Florida.

Germany

Germany invented the term "guest worker" for its immigrant laborers and is now facing the fact that a large number of highly qualified citizens are leaving Germany, primarily for America. They have lost in recent years an average of 150,000 of its citizens. Previously, Germany went through its own flood of immigrants; now it is in the top tier of industrial nations experiencing a brain drain that, for the first time since the 1950s, now exceeds the number of immigrants. The Swiss newspaper, Blick, severely criticized the "German invasion," saying they were "arrogant and rude". Many immigrants, however, say the benefits of lower taxes and pay up to three times higher than at home far outweigh the occasional xenophobic outburst. More than 18,000 Germans moved to Switzerland last year. The US was the second most popular destination with 13,245, followed by Austria with 9,309. Switzerland already has a resident German population of 170,000. Chancellor Angela Merkel's coalition government has taken credit for a thirteen month decline in the nation's unemployment. Once again it becomes a game of illusion, because if the thousands of Germany's best and brightest leave every year. So, a chain of events begins. Expert Germans go to America, Switzerland and Austria, thereby underdeveloping Germany. Uneducated Central Americans go to Germany because their governments have squandered their nation's wealth, brutally violated the civil rights of their citizens, and failed to educate them. German businessmen eagerly hire the illegals, thereby, as in the United States, causing unemployment among their own citizens. The German government no longer is obliged to pay high wages to its scientific and technological community; the German scientists who migrated to the United States are now living in Queens, New York, the Washington suburbs, Massachusetts's high tech Route 128, and Silicon Valley, California, or in Swiss hamlets. "In Germany, the principle of reward for performance doesn't exist," says physicist Michael Alexander Rübhausen. He heads up a biophysics research group at Hamburg University. The European community is learning that it now lives in a global world; so, in order to stay competitive it must invest in its own people.

LERU

One ray of hope is the establishment of *The League of European Research Universities* (LERU), founded in 2002 as an association of twelve research-intensive universities. In 2006 membership was extended to twenty institutions. Its rationale for existence is a healthy sign. It has as its premise that Europe has lost its pre-eminent position in basic research, and dedicates itself to "restore that position for the acquisition of new knowledge, for the assurance of high-quality education, for the benefit of innovation in industry, and for the enhancement of quality of life in society as a whole." I hope the church is listening, especially to the words "enhancement of quality of life in society as a whole." It acknowledges that universities, acting through professional technology-transfer offices, should become partners for industry, not-for-profit organizations, and society at large. The ideal approach is this: the Christian church throughout the world should garner its enormous resources worldwide to develop a university system throughout the Third World that is connected with industry, not-for-profit organizations, and society at large. In this manner, the church can fulfill its humanitarian, Christ-centered mission.

It is true that LERU's goal is the training of young scientists capable of building and supporting Europe's role as the leading continent of the knowledge-based 21st century world. At the same time, however, they would be creating an atmosphere that permits the young to live and flourish in the environment in which they and their ancestors formed their inimitable cultures.

Project SeaCode

One unique innovation in exploiting labor is Project SeaCode. The United States has gone as far as creating a software ship-factory which keeps Indian scientists anchored in international waters, in a kind of assembly plant which produces all manner of digital devices. Project SeaCode consists of a ship, anchored more than three miles off the coast of California (international waters), with six hundred Indian computer scientists on board, who work an uninterrupted twelve-hour daily shift for four months out at sea. The owners boast: "(It is) the price of India with the proximity of the United States.' Exploitation is the name of their game.

Will things change? Without the cooperation of the two basic constituents of any Christian society, the church and state, it will be very difficult. After all, the international corporations control the flows of money both within their own nations and abroad, and they will not stand by idly while LERU forges ahead with its project. And they will appeal to the church's "sense of humanity" to assure that the church continues to be mired down in its illusionary program for "helping the poor and undocumented." Why disturb that idyllic scene with protests against the underdevelopment caused by immigration? That would be rocking the boat.

The Dream Act

The most tempting and appealing idea that contributes to the brain drain is *The Development, Relief and Education for Alien Minors Act* ("The DREAM Act"), a bill that has been introduced several times in the United States Congress and remains on its agenda. It outlines what, at first blush, is a very generous, idealistic invitation to talented young men around the world to come to the United States and fulfill their own dreams of success and wealth. A bit disturbing is that the invitation also includes a path to those wishing to join the United States military. The military part of the bill jarred me immediately. We were beginning to recruit a mercenary army, asking young men and women from around the world to put their lives on the line to defend the

United States. We were dangling future financial incentives and citizenship to lure foreigners to do for the United States what its own citizens should be doing for it, i.e., defend the nation. For me, that threw a wrench into the whole idea. I continued to stumble at the same two immoralities imbedded in the issue. First of all, there is the question of luring to the United Sates very young talent from nations that desperately need them, while there are already many millions of sons and daughters of legal immigrants and children born in America that could benefit from the education part of the bill. Secondly, the luring to this nation and educating a large cadre of talented foreigners to enter the American work force would further depress wages in general by adding to the unemployment line. Also, and very importantly, such a bill would further devastate the American black community. There are hundreds of thousands of young bright African-Americans festering in ghettos across this country, waiting to be rescued by an enlightened government. What a slap in the face to all of them to be offering scholarships to young men and women from around the world, while allowing African-Americans to despair of ever getting a good education. How obscene of our Congress to even consider the possibility of doing such a dastardly act as passing that bill. Wakeup America and oppose this bill before it becomes a fait accompli. I call on the Christian church to address the issue. This is a moral issue of great import to the black community.

Bishop Dandala

I am happy to report that there's one light in the church darkness. AACC General Secretary Bishop Mvume Dandala and delegates from nine African countries met with a variety of government officials in Washington, D.C. on July 16, 2005. Dandala said that heads of churches in Africa instituted a program the previous year to train church leaders in monitoring good governance in their respective countries. The program is allied with NGO Church World Service's Eminent Persons Program (part of the agency's Africa Initiative). The whole idea is to provide African nations with indigenous local leaders who can stay in Africa and play key roles in resolving community issues. Bishop Dandala called for assistance not in providing Amnesty to Africans who are in America illegally, but in providing local solutions to attract the best and brightest to remain in Africa. Moses Ole Sakuda, who accompanied Bishop Dandela, said that only talented Africans who remain in their own nation can solve their own problems: "The church in Africa has solutions to the continent's many challenges and, when supported by the international community, can enhance the livelihoods of the people of Africa." He asked the international community to help in funding local higher education and professional training to retain Africa's brain trust. Dandala added, "We need an enabling environment for our thinkers, intellectuals, and scientists. Africa needs funding for higher education and professional training", not just for elementary education, but "to capacitate our thinkers and professionals... to enhance the professional capacity of African people so they have the ability to solve their own problems in their own context." Another member of the delegation to Washington, a Mr. Chaka had this to say: "We need to put the fire for Africa into U.S. churches," and encourage American churches to work together and take the lead on African concerns. Chaka said Africa "needs to be important in Iowa, not just in Washington and New York City." .

Ireland Also

Just as Germany is feeling the effects of the underdevelopment of illegal immigration, so Ireland, which has experienced great economic strides in the last decade, is gearing up to handle the same problem. In 2004 the government budget included tax relief for companies that invest in research and development and increased its funding for the state-backed Science Foundation Ireland by 62 per cent. Receiving large boosts of funding are the research sector and the fields of mathematics and earth science. William Harris, Science Foundation Ireland's director general, sets the mood. "We want to make Ireland a place that's not only friendly to scientists, but science-friendly." The new Irish initiative pleased geneticist, John Atkins. "I'm delighted to see the increase in funds for science. It's an enormous improvement from how things used to be in Ireland." When developed nations like Germany and Ireland need to dig deep into their pockets to survive economically, we know that the Third World historical problem of underdevelopment is slowly but surely creeping into the developed world. Perhaps we in the developed world will pay for the deeply exploitative sins of our fathers. The Church needs to address these sins.

The Experts Speak

Berry Newman, who was the former United States Assistant Secretary of State for African Affairs from June 2004 to April 2005, had this to say: "Africa has the potential to feed itself and feed the world but we need to raise the capacity of the rural farmers." Pointing to the future, he remarked: "Rural farming (in Africa) is a good and viable way of life and needs to be nurtured." He suggested that rural farming needs to be supported by land policy, technical assistance, and access to appropriate equipment and seeds. Once again, these are the areas that the Christian church in America should focus on and use its enormous influence in bringing about. Along the same line of thinking, Dr. Pearl-Alice Marsh, a senior professional staff person for Democratic members of the House International Relations Committee, had this to say: "There's a moral imperative that we have neglected in how we engage the world: It is important that we assist Africa in unleashing its own wealth."

Brain drain deals a double blow to weak economies, which not only lose their best and brightest, and the money spent training them, but then these same poor economies have to pay an estimated $5.6 billion a year to employ foreigners. The time to act on behalf of the poor is already in arrears, for the future is already upon us. The global information and communications technology market alone accounted for three trillion US dollars in 2006. This relentless plundering of brains in Third World countries dismantles and weakens programs aimed at training human capital in the Third World, a resource that is needed to rise from the depths of underdevelopment. It is not limited to the transfer of capital; it also entails the import of grey matter, which nips a country's nascent intelligence and future in the bud. The internationalization of scientific research companies, driven by American big business and the lavish coffers of many United States universities, continues the process of underdeveloping an already undeveloped Third and Fourth World." It is immoral to do this, so there is a desperate need on the part of the Christian church to take off its rose colored glasses and do something about it. Otherwise it is complicit in the impoverishment of the poor. The church must strip away its layers of intellectual indifference and lack of serious study in the fields of science and economics.

In closing this chapter on the brain drain, let me quote a slightly shorter version of the World Bank report of October, 2005.

"In the last 40 years, more than 1.2 million professionals from Latin America and the Caribbean have emigrated to the United States, Canada and the United Kingdom. An average of 70 scientists a day have emigrated from Latin America in the course of 40 years... A number of countries, particularly small nations in Africa, the Caribbean and Central America, have lost over 30 percent of their population with higher education as a result of migration. The Caribbean islands, where nearly all nations are English-speaking, report the world's highest brain drain. In some of these islands, 8 of every 10 university graduates have left their native countries.

The International Labor Organization (ILO) points out that the number of scientists and engineers who abandon their native countries and emigrate to industrialized nations is about one third of the number of those who stay in their native countries.

The ILO report maintains that the migration of students is a precursor of the brain drain. The Organization for Economic Cooperation and Development (OECD) reported that, at the beginning of the new millennium, a bit more than 1.5 million foreign students pursued higher studies in member states and that, of these, more than half were from non-OECD countries. Of this total, nearly half a million studied in the United States, one quarter of a million in the United Kingdom and nearly 200 thousand in Germany.

Please, Christian leaders of Europe and America, join together and save the world from this continuing ravenous, unconscionable rape of The Third and Fourth Worlds. Only you have the moral authority to do so.

Chapter Four

Illegal Immigration's Impact on America's Black Community

Whoever coined the saying that illegal immigration is a "victimless" crime needs to study the statistics. If one tracks the economic progress of African-Americans, or the lack of it, over the past century there is an unmistakable correlation with patterns of immigration. Blacks have made the greatest economic advances during periods of low immigration; the opposite is true during periods of high immigration.

African-Americans have experienced the effects of the influx of illegal immigrants first and hardest. In education, the labor market, and social services, the pressures are being felt in the black community. In the spring of 2007, immigrant rights leaders called on the American people to take part in immigration marches and demand that the Congress pass immigration reform bills. They likened this universal call to that made by the civil rights movement led by Martin Luther King. They declared that if Martin Luther King, Jr. were alive today he would be out in the streets leading the marchers. They pointed to the fact that King gave his full support to the Latino farm workers movement in California, led by the charismatic Cesar Chavez. I doubt that Mr. King would have seen the call for amnesty as a legitimate civil rights battle, for there are no civil rights involved. The call for defending civil rights revolves around American citizens, citizens who are denied rights granted to them by the American constitution. There are no such rights granted to foreigners who are here illegally, who have come here in violation of American law. It is as simple as that. To make the comparison between amnesty for illegal immigrants and rights for American-born blacks is a slap in the face to the black community that fought and struggled during the 1960s civil rights movement. As American citizens they had to fight against the racist mentality that motivated and steered even law enforcement officials. These brave and abused men and women, Americans all, were seen, even through the haze of racist ideology, as holding the moral high ground, and they became the conscience of America. To contrast them with the flood of illegal criminals that dominate the inner cities of America today is unacceptable and insulting. To contrast the efforts of well-meaning but uninformed churchmen to regularize millions of men and women who are violating the law, with the efforts of black Americans, faced with baton wielding law enforcement officials, police dogs and water cannons to assert their rights as Americans is absurd. All Americans, except for the determined, unquenchable racists, considered racial segregation immoral and indefensible. It is true that many Americans did not want to get involved in the struggle, but they did know and acknowledge in their hearts that racism had to be abolished. They did, in the end, honor Martin Luther King and his associates as American heroes. The vast majority of Americans understood that the cry of "We Shall Overcome," was an American cry that the entire world paid attention to. The dignity and civility with which Martin Luther King's civil rights movement continues to present a mirror to the face of white America is a model worthy of Mahatma Gandhi. And, just as the plight of America's black community has come to be acknowledged by all of us as unacceptable, a new danger has showed its head, that of illegal immigration. In some parts of our nation a flood of illegal immigrants who snatch jobs from both white and black Americans by working at is economically threatening the black community near-slave wages, in many cases supplementing their pittances with criminal activity. Because the black community suffered for so long, it hesitates to descry this massive foreign intrusion into their lives, their communities, their schools and their hospitals. However, it is hurting them, as they get shunted aside not only by legal immigrants but by an invasion of illegal immigrants as well

Not Something New

Historically, blacks have suffered as a result of immigration. During the decades after the revolution, free blacks occupied many jobs in the crafts, but in the 1800s the United States experienced an increase in immigration because of the Napoleonic Wars. These new immigrants looked for work. By 1820, blacks in New York City had already begun to suffer unemployment as Germans and Irish artisans supplanted them rapidly in the work place, eating away at the economic mobility enjoyed by the black population. Their displacement led to their occupying dishwashing, house servant and boot black jobs. Slowly but surely immigration began to eat away at economic mobility opportunities for blacks. No less a figure than Frederick Douglass declared: "The old employments by which we have heretofore gained our livelihood are gradually but inevitably, passing into other hands. Every hour sees the black man elbowed out of employment by some newly- arrived immigrant whose hunger and whose color are thought to give him a better title to the place." The situation today is similar. During the Civil Rights era of the 1950s and 1960s, which was to have "freed" black Americans socially and economically, Congress also changed immigration law to pave the way for close to a million legal immigrants a year, thus putting blacks once again in a precarious position. The job situation for blacks has continued to deteriorate ever since. For example, a GAO study found that a decade of heavy immigration to Los Angeles has transformed the janitorial industry from primarily unionized black workers to one of non-unionized Latinos, many of whom are illegal aliens. In California, the employment of black Americans as hotel workers decreased by 30 percent in the 1980s; during the same period, the number of immigrants with such jobs rose 166 percent. Similar situations now obtain in the garment industry, the restaurant business, hospital work, and public service jobs. The Bureau of Labor Statistics released a study claiming that immigration accounts for about 50 percent of the decline in real wages for the lowest-skilled American workers, many of whom are blacks. In his 1996 book, *The Case Against Immigration*, Roy Beck notes that:

"To review the Black side of our nation's immigration tradition is to observe African-Americans periodically trying to climb the mainstream economic ladder, only to be shoved aside each time. It is to see one immigrant wave after another climb onto and up that ladder while planting their feet on the backs of black Americans." The Christian church needs to say mea culpa because its policies of amnesty and sanctuary make it complicit in the impoverization, with all its attendant evils, of the African-American community.

A National Bureau of Economic Research paper published in September 2006 stated that immigration accounted for about a third of the decline in the employment of African-Americans over the last few decades, as well as having a severe impact on the wages of native-born black and Hispanic Americans. The U.S. Commission on Immigration Reform, chaired by the late Barbara Jordan, concluded that present immigration numbers are a source of economic injustice in America and that, therefore, America should lower its immigration rate significantly.

Since it remains a reality that young black men in the work force are 33 percent more likely to lack a high school diploma than whites, the flood of immigrants becomes a very negative force in their lives. Residual American racism comes to play here as some employers see immigrants as more reliable and hard working than native-born blacks. Anthropologists Katherine Newman and Chauncy Lennon of Harvard studied the work patterns in Harlem Between 1992 and 1999. They kept a log of the work histories of two hundred people working in fast-food restaurants in central Harlem. Eighteen percent of the population were unemployed, and about 40 percent were living below the poverty line, while 29 percent of the households in Harlem receive some form of public assistance. In restaurants, one out of fourteen Harlem residents who apply for a job will get a job. In early 1993, 73 percent of the Harlem job seekers, even after a considerable amount of trying had not found work of any kind a year after they began to seek work. The competition within Harlem has risen to a new level, in that where the low paying jobs in the service industries used to be available for the more educated, now they are not. These low paying jobs are now available and are being occupied by high school graduates rather than by school dropouts. This means that long-term welfare recipients have a tougher time beating out their competition even for these low-wage jobs.

Now, here is where the crunch for Harlemites gets even tougher. Newman and Lennon discovered that even in Harlem, African-Americans are at a disadvantage in hiring compared to Latinos and others. blacks, in Harlem, are rejected at a much higher rate than applicants from other ethnic groups with the same educational qualifications

Forty one percent of the immigrants in their sample of low-wage workers were able to find jobs within one year, while only 14 percent of native-born blacks were able to do so. Conclusion? Uncontrolled immigration is an added job market burden on unskilled blacks in competition with immigrants beyond just the wage reduction experienced by all unskilled workers, i.e., their color. Experience shows that even though central Harlem's youth are nearly all African-American, their chance of getting a job in Harlem for which a non-African-American also applies is slim. Of course, the employers say that immigrants are more appreciative and enthusiastic about their work than local youths. What they do not say is that they love paying lower wages.

Black Solidarity with Illegals Beginning to Crack

What does the black leadership in America say about this problem? Well, there has been, as already mentioned, a great reluctance on the part of the black community to criticize another segment of society that finds itself at the short end of the job market, but that solidarity vow silence is beginning to crack. It has been noted by journalists that, increasingly, the large immigrant rallies that have taken place around the nation no longer produce an automatic declaration of support from African-Americans. Although some black leaders support the protests, many African-American residents say that illegal immigrants are taking jobs from their community. Former presidential candidate Alan Keyes, also a former ambassador, made clear in a debate that black people are hurt by illegal immigration. "These elites who have been under the thumb of certain corporate interests have an interest in cheapening the price of labor in America. Do you want to know who is first hurt by that cheapened price of labor? Black folks are first hurt, as they've been hurt in the rebuilding of New Orleans, in the rebuilding of other parts of the United States that were affected by those hurricanes... I think people, including a lot of the black liberals, are more worried about what we do with illegal immigrants than they've ever been about the impact of illegal immigration on black Americans who have been in this country all along. I'm sick of seeing it."

At the debate that took place in September of 2007 at Morgan State University, a historically black school, the top four GOP presidential candidates — former Massachusetts governor Mitt Romney, former New York mayor Rudy Giuliani, Arizona Senator John McCain and former Tennessee Senator Fred Thompson — elected to absent themselves from the forum, citing scheduling conflicts. The missing candidates were represented by empty podiums. How

Republicans will be affected by this public snub is anyone's guess, but it hardly endeared them to more African-Americans. Debate moderator Tavis Smiley noted: "Some of the campaigns that declined our invitation to join us tonight have suggested publicly that this audience would be hostile and unreceptive."

Republicans Learning

But it was not all bad news for the Republicans because Smiley also said: "there are some in the Republican Party who do understand the importance of reaching out to people of color." The four candidates who skipped this debate also skipped a June forum hosted by the National Association of Latino Elected and Appointed Officials. Univision, the TV station that has a large Hispanic audience, canceled a GOP debate when McCain was the only top-tier candidate who agreed to participate. Brownback apologized for the no-shows and called it a "disgrace that they're not here." Former Representative J.C. Watts, a black Republican from Oklahoma said, "I think the best that comes out of stupid decisions like this... is that African-Americans might say, 'Was it because of my skin color?' Now maybe it wasn't, but African-Americans do say, 'It crossed my mind.'" Gingrich noted that: "African-Americans have been hurt more by the failures of government" than any other group. In the meantime, black Americans are losing jobs that traditionally were theirs for the asking. Republicans who oppose amnesty have lost a potentially large bloc of black voters led by the black activists joining Minutemen against Illegal Immigration. If the four leading Republican contenders had appeared at the debate at Morgan State University and declared their solidarity with the black community's right to job preference over illegal aliens, they could have executed a major coup d'etat, because the black community is starting to stare that problem right in the eye.

If one of those leading Republican presidential contenders had said loud and clear that they have had enough of illegal aliens continuing to drive down wages and hurt those in this country whose livelihood depends on manual labor, the activists in the black community might well have publicly supported them, since they cannot find a major democratic candidate who likely would. A Mitt Romney or Rudolph Giuliani could have pointed out that at one single placement agency alone, illegal aliens replaced over seventy black construction workers in the Katrina recovery region. Multiply that by all the employment agencies in the area and the magnitude of the problem becomes apparent. The Republicans could have capitalized on that. But, loyalty to the President overrode that great opportunity. Post 2008 election discussions will certainly bring out that obvious political miscalculation.

There is an inevitable but unavoidable downside to the black community's awakening to the fact that illegal immigration is a threat to blacks, i.e., the polarization of blacks and Latinos. The year 2006 is probably the last year that the black community will have supported illegal immigration. In May 2006, some black leaders and their supporters in Washington, D.C., calling their unity Choose Black America, held a press conference and stated unequivocally that the overwhelming majority of black Americans agreed with them that illegal immigration was the prime threat to blacks. Their platform did not go unnoticed. The Federation for American Immigration Reform paid the airfare, hotel accommodations, and expenses for members of the group. When the immigration reform bill in Congress died a quiet death, the group disappeared from the public forum. But, since President Bush expressed his determination, in spite of the setback, to ram this bill through before he left office, the group reorganized itself to do battle. But there was no battle. Bush's time had run out. It should be noted that this is not the first time that the black community has organized itself against illegal immigration. Black attitudes toward illegal immigrants, which almost always were seen as supporting illegal immigrants, were put to the electoral test in Arizona with a ballot initiative. Proposition 200 (November 16 2004): to bar illegals from receiving government assistance, forbade state money to be used, mandated tough sanctions on employers for hiring illegal immigrants, and tighter border enforcement. Exit polls showed that more than 65 percent of blacks backed the measure. As with Proposition 187, it passed by a landslide. The vote by blacks on the anti-illegal immigration ballot shows us not only their opposition to illegal immigration, but also their opposition to the support the Congressional Black Caucus has given to the passage of a comprehensive immigration reform law. It also highlighted the fact that the black community is worried about the new battle they are waging in America, the battle with illegal immigrants for jobs, since blacks have the highest rates of unemployment of any group in America. It does not help their cause any that the practice of corporate downsizing and outsourcing is accompanied by massive cuts in federal and state jobs and skills, training funds, and programs. For once at least, whites and blacks are on the same page, at the expense of black/Latino relationships. We all remember Watts, in California. It was a city controlled by the black community and the locale of some of the biggest black protests ever to take place in America. Now, Watts is 60 percent Hispanic. A row of businesses that used to employ young blacks now has signs advising that Spanish-speaking is a sine qua non of employment there. In some schools young blacks are required, if they want an education, to sit uncomprehendingly in Spanish-speaking classes. For the first time ever, in June of 2007, the first city in the United States to issue an official permit for blacks to march against illegal immigration was Los Angeles. It is true that America has a shortage of skilled workers, especially in utility companies. They need welders, plant operators and engineers if they are to prevent blackouts and electricity shortages. Quickly getting on the immigrant bandwagon, company executives back immigrant guest worker programs. They can see dollar signs as they contemplate the low wages they can pay to illegal immigrants carrying fake IDs and Social Security Numbers. In the meantime, rising unemployment devastates the African-American community. There is a simple solution to this problem that would take perhaps two to three months of training. Ad hoc, even outdoor classes could be held to train young black American and white American youth to do these jobs. Problem solved. But, that is not what the average businessman wants. That would oblige these mega-giant companies to pay living wages, and this, as they think of a possible reduction of their Xmas bonuses, is too painful to contemplate. Corporate America seeks young black employees when they cannot get illegal aliens. The Wall Street Journal reported such a case in January of 2007. After a wave of raids by federal immigration agents, a local chicken-processing company, Crider Inc., lost 75 per cent of its mostly Hispanic nine hundred-member work force. The crackdown surprised the plant ownership for, until the defeat of the proposed congressional immigration reform bill, the lack of federal enforcement of the law led them into a feeling of self-confidence that enforcement would never take place. But, once it did, they acted quickly. Crider suddenly raised pay at the plant. An advertisement in the weekly Forest-Blade newspaper announced "increased wages" at Crider, starting at $7 to $9 an hour. The African-Americans among the town's population quickly filled the breach as this unexpected opportunity presented itself, belying the canard that illegal immigrants fill job placements that Americans do not want to do.

Black Incarceration

A September 2006 working Paper 12518 of the National Bureau of Economic Research, out of Cambridge, Massachusetts had some powerful observations. The employment rate of black men, and particularly of low-skill black men, fell sharply between 1960 and 2000, while the incarceration rate of black men rose dramatically. There is an obvious correlation between immigration, black wages, black employment rates, and black incarceration rates. As immigrants began to fill jobs usually filled by unskilled whites and blacks, the wages of black workers fell, their employment rate declined, and the incarceration rate rose. The co-relationships are a no-brainer. The employment rate of African-American men fell from 74.9 percent in 1960 to 67.9 percent in 2000. Unskilled whites fared better, as their unemployment rate dropped from 87.0 to 85.2 percent during that same period. It is simple. Young black men are much more likely to be unemployed, school dropouts and prisoners than whites. While it would be naïve to ascribe this condition to only one factor, nevertheless statistical analysis does show that mass immigration is a big factor. As in any other ethnic community, other factors played a part. The changes in wage levels, especially the real wage of low-skill workers, discouraged low-skill black men from entering the labor market. .

The 1965 immigration law that saw the beginning of immigration on a very large scale was first described by the black community as a civil rights victory. The black community wanted to see itself in solidarity with other non-white communities. The immigration increase, however, once it began to reach astronomical figures (thirty million legal immigrants alone) produced negative effects on both black and white American youths. Immigration has forced down the wages of young American men who do not possess a high school degree by $1,800 a year, and increased black unemployment by a third, according to economists at Northeastern University. It is true that there are other sociological factors among black youth that helps explain higher unemployment and increased incarceration, but we must not omit the immigration effect, especially since, with the cooperation of church and state in America it is a phenomenon that can be fixed with a bit of ingenuity and effort. Unfortunately, there is no such national church initiative, but there should be. The Associated Press reported, April 30, 2007, that the son or daughter of a poor black immigrant from a Third World nation has a better chance of attending an elite American university than a young American black whose parents, grandparents and great grandparents helped build this nation with their sweat and blood! There is something wrong with this picture. Black American scholars Henry Louis Gates and Lani Guinier, two Harvard University professors, have noted that white educators are skirting around the lack of American blacks in American universities by recruiting black immigrants who look like black Americans, but are not. If this is true, then American educators need to pull up their collective socks. They need to understand that if the $10 billion that it costs American taxpayers a year to subsidize illegal aliens were spent on disadvantaged Americans, unskilled whites and blacks would be much happier. If you add to that figure the amount of money extracted by illegal Mexicans alone from our economy that ends up in Mexico, an estimated $40 billion wired to Mexico since 2006. If we add to that amount, the much larger deficits at the state and local level, where most social services to illegals are provided, we reach astronomical amounts that could, if used properly for the good of American citizens to reduce poverty, increase the ability of all young Americans to attend the finest Universities both at home and abroad, and increase medical insurance benefits for all Americans. The only group that would suffer decreased wages and decreased standard of living in this scenario would be corporate America. Don't look to see me weeping for them, because that won't happen. The interests of poor unskilled and uneducated black and white Americans are very clear: No amnesty, no guest-workers, enforce the immigration law. Period. One African-American called a spade a spade. In April 2007,

Armstong Williams, syndicated columnist, in an article titled: Are We Ready to Get Tough on Immigration? wrote: "Illegal immigration has caused enormous job displacement for American workers, infiltration of schools by non-English-speaking students, increased crime and other severe problems.

Apparently our immigration system does not work. We should send all illegal immigrants back to where they came from because this is an explosive situation just waiting to detonate..." The buzz in the black community is that although Reverends. Jesse Jackson and Al Sharpton support illegal aliens and amnesty, many African-Americans believe they do so as partisan Democrats and not in the best interests of blacks in America. If we must compare the relative apportionment of civil rights in this nation we have to conclude that the civil rights black Americans have earned after generations of struggle are far more important than extending civil rights to the very illegals who depress black wages and employment rates. We need to emphasize again and again that civil rights belong to American citizens, not illegal aliens. Human rights for illegal aliens, yes; civil rights for illegal aliens, no. To paraphrase Rev. Jesse Lee Peterson; founder and president of BOND, credibility in immigration policy can be summed up in one sentence: Immigrants who should get in let them in; immigrants who should be kept out, let them stay out; immigrants who should not be here, let them leave.

Psychological Factors in Black Unemployment

Unemployment leads to poverty; poverty can lead to stress, and stress can lead to mental health problems. Stressful, unrewarding, and demoralizing work for the working poor, together with a scarcity of the necessities and amenities of life leads to discouragement and financial instability, factors that in any family can lead to the serious dysfunction of family unity and divorce. Economically disadvantaged families often live in neighborhoods marked by high crime rates, inadequate housing, and a high proportion of teenage pregnancies and unprepared motherhood. So, it is not surprising that serious psychological problems plague such neighborhoods. Research and experience have shown that African-American women experience higher levels of economic and psychological distress than those experienced by their white counterparts. single black mothers are more likely to be poor and are at greater risk of anxiety, depression, and health problems. The church should step into the breach and defend the black community. It has the power to shame greedy, avaricious corporate executives into helping black America, their fellow Americans. In Chicago, the number of manufacturing jobs decreased by 49 percent between 1991 and 2006. Multiply that around the nation and contemplate the disastrous results for American workers, as corporate America outsources hundreds of thousands of American jobs. In 1988, General Motors closed their auto manufacturing plant in Flint, Michigan, laying-off 30,000 American workers. These jobs went to Mexico where poor foreign workers received seventy cents an hour. This move eliminated having to provide costly benefits, having to maintain safe workplace conditions, having to uphold harassment or discrimination laws, and any union interference or demands. The dehumanization of employees is the name of the game for that part of the business community that is greedy. . When a corporate executive stands up on a platform and declares that what this nation needs is a guest worker program, he is simply begging that his bonus for the current year be upped from two million to four million dollars, his Xmas gift from the workers on the plant floor, who can barely, if at all, purchase medical insurance. Congress mandates medical care and schooling for illegals even though Congress does not mandate those things for citizens who have no financial means. I have lived overseas a good many years and even among those who benefit from the U.S.'s lax rules on immigration, there is derision and laughter at America's "stupid" immigration rules. They cannot believe that a nation with so many university graduates can act so openly against its own interests. They are, however, eager to take advantage of the fact. This greed has caused a national situation in which young blacks that lack competitive technical skills and professional training are heading straight for the outer margins of American society. The only ones who can help, i.e. the Christian church, the corporate community, the Congress and the White House have joined purposefully or accidentally to deprive low income black and low income white American citizens of their daily bread. It is very disgraceful. For the church to so publicly support the immorality of illegal immigration makes it even more important that it spend more time studying the negatives. I found this report sent to me by a friend. He cannot remember where he got it from, so I apologize in advance for anyone's permission I should have received before quoting it.

"LOS ANGELES – From where Johnny Blair Vaughn sits outside Lucy Florence Coffee House in the heart of Los Angeles's black community, he can feel the temperature rising over immigration. The biggest reason, says the father of seven, is jobs. "If you drive across this city, you will see 99 percent of all construction is being done by Hispanics.... You will see no African-American males on these sites, and that is a big change," says Mr. Vaughn, who has worked in construction for two decades. His two oldest boys, in their early 20s, have been turned down so many times for jobs, that they no longer apply," he says. Echoes of Vaughn's words are rising throughout urban black America as Congress labors over immigration reform. In cities where almost half of the young black men are unemployed, a debate is raging over whether undocumented Latinos are elbowing aside blacks for jobs in stores, restaurants, hotels, manufacturing plants, and elsewhere. Hispanics and blacks tend to gravitate to the same inner-city areas and low-skill labor markets. The result is a clash over jobs that require less skill and less education, experts say. "In this era of mass immigration, no group has benefited less or been harmed more than the African-American population," says Vernon Briggs, a Cornell University professor who researches immigration policy and the American labor force. Statistics show that young African-Americans are having trouble in the job market. Unemployment and underemployment among young blacks nationwide is 40 percent, according to the US Bureau of Labor Statistics. Let us end this chapter with a prayer that the Christian church will use study and rectitude in realigning itself with the poor in all nations in such a manner as to create a true balance of legitimate dignity and prosperity. Let us pray that our Christian leadership will come to realize that with their policies and the influence they have over Congressmen, they are contributing to the decimation of the black community in America. This is immoral. Let us pray that this message reaches their heats and minds.

Blogger Comments

-Shay: Illegal immigration is a hot topic this week. With the growing rallies across America, black immigrants who went the legal route are piping up about how illegal immigration undermines black economic opportunity.

-Ed Brown, a black moderate-liberal blogger, writes: "The Senate judiciary committee released a bill that would reward illegal immigration. My father came to this country, legally, to gain employment and a chance at a better life. But he went through the process. Meanwhile, when one friend was looking for work, he decided to try day laboring. He thought it would be a good way to find out who is hiring and then try to get something more long term. He went to the 'unofficial' day labor pick up spots and tried to get a job. Guess what? He wasn't successful. Another friend works with steel. He's tried to get black men jobs but it doesn't work out. The reason? Other contractors are hiring illegal immigrants at low wages. When they bid on low cost contracts, guess who wins? So his company has to 'fight fire with fire'. This really stinks."

-Ripclawe, a Caribbean immigrant and conservative Republican who acquired U.S. citizenship, writes: "Here is the best part, a bunch of illegals protesting without fear which shows how lax American enforcement has become got the attention of the amnesty lovers. All the people like me who went thru the process of getting citizenship the right way, how stupid were we?"

-Another writes: My family has been in America since at least 1822 - the product of slavery - so I have no recent immigrant tale. However, like black moderate blogger Angela Winters and black moderate-conservative blogger Cobb, I vehemently oppose illegal immigration. It is blacks (along with legal Latinos) who bear the brunt of illegal immigration, in employment rates. And it is lower-income black communities that are often overrun first with illegal immigrants who drain social services that should go to citizens and legal residents. Los Angeles is a prime example of this point. If black folks must follow the law, then no special rights for anyone else. And no way should illegal immigrants immediately get rights that took centuries for blacks to acquire. Especially when amnesty-in-disguise proposals will only increase illegal immigration, as it did when President Ronald Reagan tried it.

Nor do I buy the "illegal immigrants do jobs that Americans don't do" argument. Who do you think were doing these jobs beforehand? Who do you think often still does them, in areas with few illegal immigrants? Nor do illegal immigrants only do the so-called crappy jobs; they are also in areas like construction. Illegal immigrants undermine the wages of low-income black (and other) workers, thus undermining the economic opportunity of lower-income blacks (and others) even further. I have no issues with legal immigration, but I have a huge problem when folks want to illegally get over folks' backs, while pimping off our rich civil rights history to try to get there.

-Dan the Highway guy:

One disagreement I might have with your post is when you say:

"If black folks must follow the law, then no special rights for anyone else. And no way should illegal immigrants immediately get rights that took centuries for blacks to acquire." If something is actually a human right, injustice done to people in the past should have no bearing on according them to people in the future. However, I would probably be right in assuming that what you are referring to here are things that I wouldnot call 'rights.' Without putting words in your mouth, these might be things like state support, living wage, health and childcare. I don't consider these things to be 'rights.'

For Ordering Additional Copies of On The Immorality of Illegal Immigration By Father Patrick Bascio (Revised Edition)

On-Line Orders: Go to ***AuthorHouse.com***. Click on ***Bookstore*** to enter bookstore browser. Enter ***Bascio*** in the search window of the bookstore browser. When the Bascio book image appears click on ***Add to Cart***. Then click on ***Proceed to Checkout*** and provide information on number of copies needed, shipping address and method, billing information, and credit card information for payment to complete order. Address e-mail inquiries to customersupport@authorhouse.com

Telephone Orders: Dial Author House Book Sales toll free at 1-888 519-5121 Extension 5023 or 1-888 280-7715. Have ready Bascio book title and ISBN number (ISBN 9781449001858) and credit card information for customer support representative who will assist you. The general purpose toll-free number for Author House books is 1-800 839-8640

Mail Inquiries: Address all mail inquiries about book purchases with name address and phone number to:

Customer Support
Author House Books
Suite 1663 Liberty Drive, Suite 200
Bloomington, IN 47403

Book Store Purchases: *On the Immorality of Illegal Immigration,* by Father Patrick Bascio (ISBN 9781449001858), can also be ordered through major bookstores and through amazon.com.

Chapter Five

Americans Will Do the Work

You have heard it before: "The jobs Americans won't do". This is the phrase we constantly hear from those who want to keep our borders unchecked, whatever their motivation. Their passion makes use of false or uninformed piety and false or uninformed religious sentiment. President Bush led the way. He constantly spoke of "jobs Americans are not doing." The president was either kidding or deceiving. Those Americans who line up for jobs everyday, jobs that they see illegal aliens walking away with, would not echo his statement. A notorious case of open-border spin is the case of Cindi Smallwood who claimed she could not find workers to dig ditches even at $34 an hour. There is something suspicious here. You see, Cindi Smallwood was president of the Orange County chapter of the California Landscape Contractors Association, and a member of the association's "immigration task force." She opposed the punitive Immigration Reform Bill proposed by Rep. James

Sensenbrenner. His measure stressed border enforcement to the exclusion of comprehensive immigration reforms, emphasized sanctions on employers, and opposed re-entry for any reason of illegals that are deported. Many observers say that her language is a kind of doublespeak in that she uses the language of the opponent of illegal immigration to push illegal immigration. Machiavelli would have been proud of her. Smallwood is actually a supporter for the open-borders lobby. She certainly has a right to be that if she wishes. I guess it's just the stealth manner in which she operated that was a bit disconcerting. Her claim of not being able to find anyone who would cut lawns in the sun for 34 dollars an hour was quickly seized upon by Congressman Jim Kolbe, a strong supporter of the comprehensive bill that fell short of support in the 2007 Congressional debate. In a speech, he said: "Cindy Smallwood, owner of a landscaping business, was recently interviewed on television after searching in vain for employees to fill a $34 per hour job. That's hardly low-paying work. Thirty-four dollars an hour, and no takers, at least not from anyone remotely qualified. She just couldn't interest Americans to do the backbreaking work that her business requires. That's just one employer, but multiply that by millions of small businesses all across the United States and you begin to see signs of a looming economic crisis."

What the congressman may not have known is that Cyndi Smallwood appeared on the John and Ken Show. She told them that after the article appeared in the LA Times she received over thirty resumes in just a few hours time for a job that she claimed no Americans would do. I would like to give the good Congressman the benefit of the doubt and believe that he really believes that it is difficult, if not impossible, to find an American that would be willing to cut a lawn in the sun for $34 an hour. However, that is a stretch. Laura Ingraham featured Ms Smallwood on her radio show and, in less than a minute she had three qualified Americans that were ready and willing to work for her for at $34.00 an hour. Just as dramatically Ms. Ingraham received four hundred emails requesting a job from Ms Smallwood. Some of the callers were even willing to relocate from the east coast. It sounds more like desperation to get a bill passed than it does of a great fear that the American economy is about to collapse.

And, as for Ms. Smallwood, at the time she made her remarks she had twelve employees, and she says that all are in the country legally. If we put that into the context of her statement that without a guest worker program, her company probably would not survive, then, she should have been out of business a long time ago. Her argument that we must have, in effect, open borders so that she would be able to hire eight employees at $34 an hour, is a smokescreen. What contractors, including Ms.Smallwood, really want is to be able to hire cheap labor. Is there anyone out there who is willing to mow lawns in California, where extensive lawns showcase the property of the rich, the powerful, and the Hollywood stars?

Bisbee, Arizona

The illegal invasion is so great that the invaders seemingly trip over one another as they walk through the old copper-mining town turned artist colony of Bisbee Arizona (pop. 6,000), five miles from the Mexican border. Having eluded the U.S. border patrol, they arrive in small groups of three or four, larger contingents of more than a dozen and sometimes groups of a hundred. Worried citizens who spot them keep the Bisbee police officers and Cochise County sheriff's deputies busy tracking down all the trespassing aliens. At night, as many as one hundred persons will take over a vacant house. Some crowd into motel rooms, even storage-compartment rental units. During the day, they congregate on school playgrounds, roam through backyards and pass in and out of apartment buildings. Some assemble at the Burger King, waiting for their assigned drivers to appear. Sometimes stolen cars are waiting for them, keys on the floor. But most continue walking to designated pickup points beyond Bisbee, where they will ride in thousands of stolen vehicles, often with the seats ripped out to accommodate more human cargo, on the next leg of their journey to big cities and small towns from California to North Carolina. As of 2006 an estimated 8 per cent of America's labor population was composed of illegal immigrants, while eight million U.S. citizens could not find employment, and 36 to 42 percent of illegal aliens were on welfare. For a good proportion of these people, the American dream ended up as a life of crime and welfare, while American sovereignty took another major blow. Have you been to an airport recently? If you want to reach your plane you first must show a photo ID to prove that you are who you say you are. Then you must line up for the baggage check. First you remove your shoes, then take off any clothing or belt that covers your basic attire, empty your pockets of anything metallic, including the spare change you are going to use to pick up a newspaper or buy a candy bar. Then your laptop must be separated from any other luggage and tested to find out whether or not it contains any explosive device that could down a plane. During the time it took for you to reach the airport, go through this security check and then wait to board your plane, perhaps as many as three thousand illegal aliens have crossed our borders without as much as a letter of recommendation, and certainly no document allowing them to pass. They just take a leisurely Sunday afternoon walk. No searches for weapons. No shoe removal. No photo-ID. And, chances are you are only flying from Boston to Topeka, Kansas. But it is going to get 'better' than that. These same folks who walk across our borders during their leisurely afternoon stroll without being required to take off their shoes will soon be loaded with documents. They may even have your Social Security Number, and a driver's license. Then, if they want to travel around the United States by air they will have to take their shoes off at the airport, just as you have to do. That's a consolation prize for you. Since 1970 immigration has increased the number of unskilled job applicants faster than the number of skilled job applicants. Economics 101 predicts that increasing the relative number of unskilled workers will depress wages, because employers will not need to raise wages to attract applicants for unskilled jobs. Nonetheless, those who favor an expansive immigration policy continue to insist that unskilled immigrants take jobs that natives do not want. This is sometimes true, but only in a relative sense. The reason is not that natives reject demeaning or dangerous work. Natives in Detroit and Philadelphia do almost every job that an immigrant does in Los Angeles or New York. When natives turn down such jobs in New York or Los Angeles, the reason is that by local standards, because of the influx of illegals, the wages are abysmal. Far from proving that immigrants have no impact on natives, the fact that American-born workers sometimes reject jobs that immigrants accept reinforces the claim that immigration has depressed wages for unskilled work. There are about thirty four million low-wage workers in the labor force, so there is absolutely no shortage of low-skilled workers; it is the oversupply of from nine to twelve million illegal immigrants that needs to be tackled. The notion that there is a shortage of unskilled, low-educated workers in the United States is a joke. On the contrary, the evidence shows that there is a surplus of such workers both nationwide and statewide.

Lack of Enough Training

The lifetime earnings of adults without high school diplomas over the past twenty-five years have declined dramatically, resulting in a greater demand for now-strained public services. If there is a serious problem it is that we are not training young Americans to qualify for well paying technical work, work that many illegal aliens know how to do. A good example of this is in the roofing industry. Jobs there draw $25 -$30 per/hour. That is good money, and it is earned by young illegal aliens who are trained in roofing. Our government and our church needs to learn a few things about labor conditions in our nation if they want to help the American poor. I spoke with a number of roofers from Georgia who said that they are not the only industry that has difficulty finding qualified young Americans (as opposed to unwilling). They point to the same problem fellow-employees have in the agriculture and hospital industries. The impact of this displacement of native-born workers and legal immigrants by illegals was concentrated among young Americans, especially young male and female workers without four-year college degrees. More young men suffer from this situation than do young women, especially young black and Hispanic males who live here legally. And why is this? A general consensus among employers is that there is far too much insistence that young people go to college. A young man or young woman can build a fine life being a skilled carpenter, plumber, roofer, computer technician, and repairing and building fences, landscaping, painting and a wide range of electrician skills, to name a few. Both church and state could gather their own immense resources to see to it that such training is done with students who are either financially or temperamentally unsuited for college. That is an alternative, not a disgrace. These skills are desperately needed to keep a technological society humming. People who have such skills are very valuable to America. Governor Arnold Schwarzenegger understands this and is doing something about it. He launched a "Career Technical Education (CTE) initiative in California that has great promise. His 2007-2008 budgets contained $52 million dedicated to training in all the technical areas enumerated here. Kudos for the Governor.

Statistics

-Nearly 17 million Americans are unable to find full-time jobs in the current economy. — Bureau of Labor Statistics (BLS, June 2009)

- The unemployment rate among the twelve million American adults who do not have a high school diploma is almost 15.5 percent. — (BLS, June 2009)

- Forty percent of working-age African-American men are unemployed or out of the labor force

Jobs Americans won't do?

-Seventy nine percent of the 23 million workers in service jobs are native-born Americans*.

-Eighty one percent of the 6 million workers in construction jobs are native-born Americans.

-Seventy seven percent of the 10 million workers in production jobs are native-born Americans.

*These statistics have changed since the 2009 recession.

Illegal Cash Hurts Mexican Economy

The nations that encourage their surplus labor to go abroad receive a bonus of remittances derived from their nationals who are working abroad. This has, as we have seen, the negative effects of, in the example of Mexico, wealthy Mexicans failing to invest in their own nation. The influx of Mexican-unearned cash "drives up real estate prices, stimulates conspicuous consumption of imported goods, and is unevenly distributed." So the source country earns capital temporarily but loses many emigrant workers permanently, further impoverishing it. If the opposite were true, Mexico would develop from the ground up, with development producing a wide range of needed technological skills, a necessary condition for economic progress in any nation. But, the lure of quick cash becomes a reason for Mexico to join the hidden but developing surge of One World economic measures. Having become accustomed to live off the dole of remittances sent to them by Mexican nationals working in America, the Mexican ruling class will do whatever it takes to subvert and agitate against any movement in the United States that wishes to shut down illegal immigration. They are so desperate to hide their secret war against U.S. interests that they encourage Mexican immigrants to "agitate against the United States, with the collusion of Mexican officials." These are the same officials that provide survival kits to their nationals about to cross our borders illegally while criticizing U. S. immigration policies. Unless the Mexican government steps up to the plate and reorganizes its corrupt and inefficient use of state monies and talent, Mexican citizens will never be able to have a fulfilling life. Nor can the Mexican government take pride in itself by simply pushing the poor from their house to our house. That is neither Christian charity nor respect for its citizenry. The Mexican ruling elite is trying to con America into taking on board what the Mexican government considers to be excess baggage. One day they will be called to account for disrespecting their own people in this cold and calculating manner. The Mexican bishops would be wise to take a closer look at Mexican resources. If they do, there is plenty of fodder there for pricking the consciences of the Mexican ruling class. Although half the nation's citizens live in dire poverty, Mexico is rich enough to finance enormous improvements in education and infrastructure that would give the opportunity of millions of Mexicans to lead a much better life. However, wealthy Mexicans are not very interested in spreading the wealth. They love it when their poor are able to scrap a living out of the remittances their relatives send home from the United States. That relieves them...they believe...of the burden of providing jobs for their own countrymen. When Mexican President Vicente Fox said that the Mexicans living in the United States should receive free health care, what he was really thinking of were all of those remittances from American that guaranteed the continuation of a healthy corrupt life for the Mexican elite. He made no mention of the fact that 10 out of the 26 billionaires living in Latin America were Mexicans. Prof. George Grayson of William and Mary College writes that Mexico is an "immensely wealthy nation." In the Mexican 1994 presidential election, Presidente Salinas "encouraged" a number of rich businessmen to write $25 million checks, each, for his campaign.

"Guest Workers."

This is a term that we need to come to terms with. The references is to those who come to the United States at the invitation of our government, at the request of one business establishment or another, only to be offered wages that are so low that, indeed, many Americans cannot, will not, accept them. These guestworkers are given temporary jobs, forced to live in squalid conditions; and denied medical benefits for injuries. Many of them enter already-overcrowded medical facilities and are treated at the expense of American taxpayers, leaving the employers with more money and the American taxpayers with less. There is, in other words, a systematic abuse of workers under the H-2 system (visas for temporary work permits), created and administered by the U.S. Department of Labor in 1943, and revised by Congress in 1986 to include non-agricultural workers. So, when a president says that illegals are only taking jobs that Americans won't do, what the president is really saying is that employers are justified in hiring illegals, thus depressing the wages of Americans to such a low level that it is not worth getting out of bed in the morning to enter the world of humiliation and slave labor created by the hiring of illegals. Employers in 2005 "imported" more than 121,000 temporary H-2 guestworkers, 32,000 H-2A workers for agricultural work and 89,000 H-2B workers for jobs in forestry, seafood processing, landscaping, construction and other non-agricultural industries. Then there are those who work in slaughterhouses, chicken pot pie factories, or pig farms. Before the "guestworker" program was initiated, Americans held all of these jobs at living wages. So, the argument that "illegals" and "guestworkes" do jobs that Americans will not do is a big lie and a huge injustice foisted on the American people by a government persuaded by big business interests and blessed by the lack of economic savy on the part of the church. Greedy business owners offer slave wages and squalid living conditions to foreigners, while at the same time depressing the wages of American citizens. Yet church and state still proclaim that illegals and guestworkers "take jobs that Americans will not take." Ridiculous.

In a hard-hitting report issued by the Southern Poverty Law Center, titled, "Close to Slavery: Guest Worker Programs in the United States" the story is told of a group of Thai workers who alleged that a company held them captive and sometimes watched over them with guns in North Carolina and New Orleans, where they were transported to help demolish flooded buildings after Hurricane Katrina. In another report, twelve Guatemalan guest workers were allegedly held captive and then forced to work eighty hours a week in a Connecticut nursery field for $3.75 an hour before deductions for telephone service and other costs. Church and state would have much more credibility if they insisted that all workers get a living wage, or insisted that the U.S. shut down the thousands of sweatshops spread from Maine to California, a nice no-man's land where corporations offer jobs "that Americans will not take." Perhaps they could insist that our government penalize foreign governments that allow Export Processing Zones, as in El Salvador, which have a horrific record of worker abuse and exploitation. Perhaps the Bishops' Conference of Central America might say at least a word of criticism of the Salvadoran government for failing to enforce laws against a wide variety of abuses, and failing to defend the rights of unions to collective bargaining.

Middle Class Hit

As noted by Frosty Wooldridge in "Our Country Coming Undone," illegal immigration hurts both America's poor and its middle class. Illegal immigrants compete for jobs normally done by America's poor and competition for skilled jobs by illegal immigrants has never been greater and continues to skyrocket. Government rules on immigration continue to be bent out of shape by almost all government agencies, each seemingly trying to outdo the number of both unskilled and skilled illegals. The Bush administration was able to short-circuit advances made by the Congress to curb, control or deport illegal aliens by use of a number of stealth presidential powers. As a result, illegal immigration is skyrocketing. The massive illegal immigration that has taken place since the 1960s has cut deeply into the pockets and lifestyle of America's middle-class.

That America has an illegal-immigration problem is recognized among all sides in the Immigration debate gripping the political scene. Some say there are ten million illegals in America; some say there are twenty million. The truth probably lies somewhere in-between. Standing in sharp contrast are those who want all illegals deported as soon as possible, and those who propose a form of amnesty coupled with increased immigrant quotas. No one expects an OK Corral style roundup of millions of illegal immigrants, but legalization of their status would only spur a flood of more illegal immigrants. So, what to do? First of all, it would be nothing new if we legalized their status. We did that already. In the 1980s, 2.7 million illegal aliens were legalized, and it failed to stop the flood. In fact, legal immigration has doubled since the 1980s, but we have three times as many illegals. We are treading water. If legalization solved most of the problems connected with illegal immigration, that would be one thing, but even legalized immigrants are available in such abundance that the least educated American-born workers already face stiff job competition from the many millions of legalized illegal aliens. Letting illegals stay on is only magnifying the problem. That American workers should suffer an increase in their inability to house, feed and clothe their families because of the corruption and illegality that surrounds illegal immigration is immoral. According to the FBI, South Carolina officials raided a prostitution ring that was involved in the exploitation of illegal aliens. Four people were charged with "keeping, maintaining, controlling, supporting, employing, harboring illegal aliens for the purpose of prostitution," We have to admit that this is an example of jobs that Americans have done for a very long time and likely still do.

Kathy McKee

In an article written by Kathy McKee, the state coordinator of Citizens against Illegal Immigration, as well as director of Protect Arizona NOW, Ms McKee assailed certain false assumptions. The article was published in The Sonoran News, January 4, 2004. Ms. McKee is a former Quaker Sunday school teacher and Volunteer of the Year in a large metropolitan area, with a thirty five year record of charity work and philanthropy benefiting minorities. She points out:

1. It is not racist to call these people "illegal aliens." "Illegal aliens" is the only term used in federal laws and regulations to describe those who come into our country illegally. They are not illegal immigrants, not undocumented immigrants, not migrant workers, and not day laborers – they are illegal aliens.
2. Mexico is not a poor country. It has more resources per square mile than the U.S. and plenty of money to take care of its own people. It is part of the North America Free Trade Agreement (NAFTA) with the US and Canada. This fact has driven its export-led

economy. In all of Latin America, Mexico has the highest per-capita income level. Goldman Sachs predicted that Mexico will be a leader in the world economy by 2050, along with China, Japan, US, Brazil and India.

3. Illegal aliens are not doing work Americans won't do. What jobs won't Americans do? In most states, Americans still clean their own houses, do their own landscaping, clean hotel rooms, work in restaurants and fast food places, paint houses, do construction work, work in airports, etc. That was the case for two hundred years before our government allowed these people to cross our borders virtually unchallenged. There are eighteen million Americans who cannot find a job for the simple reason that these jobs are taken by illegal aliens.
5. Illegal aliens do not contribute more than they cost. Certainly the millions of illegals in prison and on welfare are not contributing, and the ones who are working often are paid in cash with no deductions for taxes at all. The ones who use fraudulent social security numbers and qualify to pay taxes and social security have so many deductions that they pay little if any taxes. The Center for Immigration Studies estimates that the average Mexican illegal alien costs U.S. taxpayers $55,000 each over their lifetimes.

6. The economy does not depend on illegal aliens. Even though greedy CEOs (making $50 to $150 million a year) fill their coffers on the backs of illegal aliens. The only thing illegal aliens are contributing to is the collapse of our economy and making the rich richer.
7. Without illegal aliens, the price of agricultural products and other goods and services would not soar. The definitive study on this subject is the University of Iowa's "How Much Is That Tomato?" The study concludes that "since labor is such a small component of the end-price of agricultural products (which includes price to the growers, transportation costs, processing /storage costs, grocers' profit, etc.), using minimum wage workers instead of illegal aliens would increase prices of agricultural products by approximately 3 percent in the summer and 4 percent in the winter... hardly the making of $10 heads of lettuce, $25 hamburgers, $1,000 per night Days Inn hotel rooms like the pro-illegal alien lobby claims."
8. Consumers are not benefiting from lower labor costs. The Big Three automakers say they moved so many jobs to Mexico because their labor costs are 80 percent less than in America. Has this contributed to the lowering of automobile prices? No it has not.
9. One common argument for immigration is that American society is aging. We are told that we need young workers. But demogra-

> phers have found that immigration actually has only a small impact on this problem. The 2000 Census showed that 66.2 percent of the population was of working age (15 to 64). If all post-1980 immigrants (legal and illegal) and their U.S.-born children are not counted, the working-age share would still have been 65.9 percent in 2000. Ninety seven percent of illegal aliens take jobs that Americans want and need.

Third Way Attrition

Frustration at the problems connected with illegal immigration prompts some to propose what has become known as the "Third Way", i.e. attrition through enforcement. It is appealing at the theoretical level, but at a more practical level has a built-in naiveté. The Third Way advocates tell us that if America becomes less hospitable to illegals, many more will simply decide to go home, and the problem will simply go away. The proponents of this theory also suggest that if the US places very severe penalties on companies and company owners that hire illegal immigrants, this would be an additional reason for illegal immigration to eventually disappear totally or be small enough not to be a matter of concern. Every statistic makes such a proposal pie in the sky when you die. To give you an example of the unrealistic nature of attrition-through-enforcement, in 2004, only three out of many thousands of employers were fined for hiring illegals. The Internal Revenue Service must also stop accepting Social Security numbers that it knows are bogus, and there is absolutely no sign whatsoever that that will happen. So, attrition through enforcement is dead upon arrival.

Drivers' Licenses

We also need to make a much greater effort to deny illegal aliens drivers licenses, bank accounts, loans, in-state college tuition, etc. There is no way that is going to happen so long as many states are proposing to allow illegal aliens to have automobile licenses. More to the point, in October of 2005, Jessica Vaughan, Senior Policy Analyst, Center for Immigration Studies, spoke to the Massachusetts Legislature about the latest standards and procedures to ensure the integrity of driver's licenses and non-driver identification cards issued in Massachusetts. These licenses and cards issued to temporary foreign visitors would expire at the end of the visitor's stay in the United States, so they could not be used to mask their illegal status, while at the same time allowing legitimate long-term temporary visitors, such as foreign students, guest workers and journalists, to receive licenses. Ms. Vaughan explained that the key ingredients to a secure license are: a legal presence requirement, a state residency requirement, verification of key identity documents, a biometric identifier, and linking the expiration of the license to a foreign visitor's authorized duration of stay. This provision was important because visa overstayers represent a large share of the eleven to twenty million illegal aliens residing in the United States. For example, under current law, if a foreign student is admitted for a two-year degree or certificate program, if that student were to drop out of the program (invalidating the student visa) under current law, he could retain the license and use it to obtain illegal employment or pursue other activities, including terrorism. For an illegal alien, the driver's license is the next best thing to a green card -- it is a widely accepted document that allows them to function as if they were here legally. Far more than mere permission to drive, the license facilitates employment and enables the bearer to board airplanes and trains, rent cars or trucks, wire money overseas, enter government buildings, and purchase a gun in some states.

Licenses Are Coveted by Terrorists.

All of the 9/11 hijackers had driver's licenses or non-driver identification cards, and the National Commission on Terrorist Attacks noted that obtaining the documents was a key step in the ultimate success of the operation. A significant proportion of terrorists who operated in this country between the early 1990s and 2004 used valid temporary visas to enter the United States. This includes six of the nineteen 9/11 hijackers. Many also overstayed their visas, including Mohammed Atta, the ringleader. Under current law, individuals like these would have access to a full-term license. The Registry of Motor Vehicles should issue licenses and identification cards only to those visitors who already have been vetted by these agencies. Through the visa issuance or formal admissions process the validity of the state-issued document can be restricted to the period of time authorized by the federal agency. To fail to take this precaution is to invite fraud and abuse and compromise national security.

Who is Responsible?

While the regulation of immigration is a federal responsibility, it is largely the state governments that pay the price for federal policy or enforcement failures. Thus states have a have a big role to play, and a legitimate interest, in helping the federal government address the problems. Maintaining prudent and sensible driver's licensing standards is one of the most important things a state can do to contribute to the effort to limit illegal immigration and prevent future terrorist attacks. Sometimes it seems that the only people who are expected to comply with the immigration law are nominees for cabinet posts. Unfair as that may seem, Bernard Kerik's illegal-alien nanny at least forces us to confront the absurdity at the center of our immigration policy. On the one hand, we have laws that appear tough, banning the employment of illegal aliens, for instance. This is done to satisfy public concerns over uncontrolled borders and mass immigration. The absurdity lies in the fact that these laws are almost never enforced. This is a national disaster in that it saddles the middle class with new taxes, undermines assimilation and makes it easier for terrorists to enter our country. It wouldn't even reduce illegal immigration, since foreigners who didn't qualify under new rules would understand that all they have to do is go nowhere, that those who do the hiding of illegals will eventually convince enough congressmen that they pass another bill that favors illegals.

The other approach is to start enforcing the law. This is an attainable goal, for immigration is not an uncontrollable force of nature. It is driven mainly by the economy and sparked and nurtured by government policies. During the last two decades illegal immigration began to substantially increase and average hourly wages for American male workers with less than a high school education declined more than 20 percent relative to inflation. The National Academy of Science reported in "Dropping Out – Immigrant Entry and Native Exit from the Labor Market, 2000-2005" that from 1980 to 1995 there was a 44 percent decline in the real wages of high school dropouts as a result of immigration. It is the height of hypocrisy to raise the minimum wage on the one hand while the other hand willfully allows the massive importation of illegal immigrants who will work at barely life-sustaining wages. It is immoral, an immorality that is shameful in a publicly acknowledged Christian nation. The American worker and taxpayer are victims.

The only "evidence" of a labor shortage comes from the very employers who artificially create one so that they can make even more money than they already do, from illegal labor. In addition to harming the poorest and least educated American workers, our immigration system has created a large burden for taxpayers. The best predictor of poverty and welfare dependence in modern America is the education level. Given the low educational levels of most recent immigrants, we would expect them to be a greater drain on public coffers than the immigrants who came before them. Indeed this is the case. In 1997 the National Academy of Sciences (NAS) estimated that immigrant households consumed $20 billion more in public services than they paid in taxes each year. Adjusted for inflation, with the current size of the immigrant population today, this figure would be over $40 billion. There are approximately five million illegal workers who are collecting wages on a cash basis and are avoiding both income and FICA taxes. The United States is hooked on cheap, illegal workers.

In New Bedford, Massachusetts

On Tuesday, March 6, 2007, three hundred federal immigration agents raided a New Bedford, Massachusetts leather manufacturer at a factory that produced handbags and leather goods, including military backpacks and survival vests. Since 2003, it had received almost a million dollars in defense contracts, and its workforce grew from eighty-five to five hundred. They took into custody the company's owner and three managers on charges that they hired illegal workers to labor at military contracts worth millions of dollars. Three hundred fifty illegal employees were taken into custody and taken to Fort Devens for processing, three hundred fifty out of a total labor force of five hundred. Most of them were of Hispanic origin, forced to work under deplorable conditions. The management not only were fully aware of the documentation presented by the illegals, they even gave them lessons on how to obtain fake documents. Except for fingerprint readers or retinal scans, all lesser documentation can be forged. The children of those detained were left in Massachusetts, much to the ire of the Department of Social Services. They had not been notified of the impending raid and, as a consequence, were not prepared for a sudden influx of children that had to be cared for. Most of the children had no idea of the location or condition of their parents.

The Notorious Matriculas Consulares

The Matrícula Consular (Consular Registration) is an identification card issued by the Government of Mexico through its consulate offices to prove that the bearer is a Mexican national living outside of Mexico. It includes an official Government of Mexico issued ID number and bears a photograph and address of the Mexican national to whom it is issued. However, it is totally not needed. What a Mexican national legally residing in the United States should have is a valid Mexican passport and a valid U.S. Visa, or a U.S.-issued "Green Card" (I-551 form). Its very use is a sign that the one using it is in the United States illegally. In other words, the Mexican government is openly, without embarrassment and without any reproof from the United States government, providing documentation with the purpose of assisting its citizens to illegally and permanently live in the United States. Similar consulate identification cards are issued to citizens of Argentina, Colombia, El Salvador,

Honduras, and Peru. The tri-border region of South America (where Argentina, Paraguay, and Brazil intersect) is recognized as a "hotbed of Islamic fundamentalism." And, in spite of this, the Congress sits on its thumbs whistling, of all songs, "Dixie."

On September 14, 2004 Congress voted down a motion to prevent financial institutions from accepting consular IDs. But do you think it is only the Congress that is doing so? Surprise! Even some states and municipalities allow the Matrícula Consular as an official form of identification. Matricula Consulares are accepted as a form of ID by most major U.S. banks and by Texas local government entities, six Texas counties, 22 cities and 16 Texas police departments. All of this, in spite of the fact that Matrícula Consular cards are issued by Mexican Consulates without checking the authenticity of the applicant's supporting documentation. Mexican nationals often provide birth certificates to their consular authorities but, in fact, Mexican birth certificates are easily forged and can be purchased on the black market for a few dollars.

More about the Matriculas Consulares

The banks, of course, who love to accept money from illegals and never meet an illegal they do not like, accept the cards as a form of ID. Now, the ordinary Joe, like you and I, i.e. most Americans, no matter what we say, no matter our outcry, we can do nothing about it. That is democracy? I don't think so. The bankers sound so nice when they appear to be concerned about the "convenience of our customers."

How? Well, they say, Matriculas Consulares make it easier for Mexicans in the United States to open bank accounts. They are so kind. As for concerns about security and terrorist activities, the bankers say that federal laws governing suspicious transactions give law enforcement authorities the necessary tools. The bankers must have been very upset when the FBI's Pat Patterson, special agent, San Antonio office, thought that these IDs are not a good idea at all. He points out that any person in the United States legally either has a green card or can get a passport. That is no big deal. Instead, an estimated (as of March 25, 2004) 2 million illegal immigrants are using these very questionable Mexican-issued IDs. A passport can be electronically scanned; a Matricula Consulares cannot. It can also easily be obtained, fraudulently, and even duplicated so that one person can own several of them, each containing a different name. A terrorist could easily obtain a driver's license simply by using this form of ID. At least 24 states accept this ID when one is applying for a driver's license, and once a driver's license is issued in one state that accepts Matriculas Consulares, it can be transferred to another state that does not. A terrorist using this ID can also board a plane with no questions asked. This is happening in spite of the fact that in testimony to the Senate Judiciary Committee, the FBI reported that the Matrícula Consular card is unreliable as an identification card and is highly vulnerable to fraud. An FBI spokesperson worried: "As the use and concept of the 'MCAS' gains acceptance, the threat of countries hostile to the U.S. or those known to sponsor terrorist organizations issuing said cards is potentially greater." One tiny light in this darkness was that the U.S. government does not accept Matricula Consulares as a form of ID for entering federal buildings. Or does it? To test to what extent authorities were protecting us from terrorists, Bruce DeCell, a retired New York City police officer who lost a son-in-law in 9/11, got hold of a forged Matrícula with his name. He was able to enter the Department of Homeland Security with it. He bought the card from a street vendor in California. Just to see how sharp this bastion of American security was, he gave as his address "123 Fraud Blvd." in "Staten Island", New York, and his birthplace as "Tijuana", B.C. All of this sounds like a bad dream, but it is an ever-present reality.

Braceros

What is a Bracero? A bracero is a Latin American migratory worker slipping into our southwestern states looking for work, especially when it came time of year for the cotton crop to be picked. They got work, but spent a good part of their wages just barely surviving. Their upkeep was (is) minimal as they harvest the crop, and then say adios until the next cotton picking season arrived. Generally speaking, the Latin American migratory worker going into west Texas is regarded as a necessary evil, nothing more nor less than an unavoidable adjunct to the harvest season. Judging by the treatment that has been accorded him in that section of the state, one might assume that he is not a human being at all, but a species of farm implement that comes mysteriously and spontaneously into being, coincident with the maturing of the cotton. It is an instrument that requires no upkeep or special consideration during the period of its usefulness, needs no protection from the elements, and when the crop has been harvested, vanishes into the limbo of forgotten things - until the next harvest season rolls around. The bracero had no past, no future, only a brief and anonymous present. Back in the '60s, César Chávez and his United Farm Workers union won a 40 percent wage increase in the San Joaquin Valley of California, and the use of braceros was discontinued. Those were good days for farm workers, but that economic improvement was nullified as illegals began to flood the area, offering to work at low wages. Ironically, the farmer continues to report difficulties in acquiring labor to harvest their crops, even though the unemployment rate in the Central Valley of California is exceptionally high. It is an outright lie that the farmers cannot find American workers; they can, but do not want to pay a living wage. American jobs in farming are a function, not of the availability of American workers; it is a function of the invasion of our farming communities by illegals from Mexico and, through Mexico, other nation of South America. Period. While we send troops to Iraq to defend its borders from an illegal invasion from Iran or Saudi Arabia, a fight that is not ours to make, we have no troops and no will to guard our southern borders from the invasion orchestrated by and permitted by the Mexican government. There is something wrong with this scenario. Almost no one in public life wants to admit the disastrous results of either the bracero program or the 1986 amnesty program that was supposed to end the invasion of illegal immigrants altogether. That became just another pipe dream in the bureaucratic maze. Half of our government is failing to act efficiently to protect us and the other half is working efficiently not to protect us. We are in bad shape. The fact is that as illegals solidify their presence in this country, they move on to better jobs in other parts of our economy, leaving space in agriculture for more illegals to replace them. In the meantime, the young American cannot find work.

How Ike Dealt with the Problem

George W. Bush did not stand alone as a Republican president who had to face the problem of the porous US-Mexican border. Over fifty years ago, when newly elected Dwight Eisenhower moved into the White House, America's southern frontier was as porous as a sieve. Three million illegal migrants poured across sour borders looking for jobs in Texas, California and Arizona. Eisenhower acted swiftly and decisively to stop this invasion of our borders. He did so with only 1,075 United States Border Patrol agents - less than one-tenth of today's force. His forthright reaction to violations of American territory is still praised by veterans of the Border Patrol. In 1951, Ike wrote a letter to Sen. William Fulbright (D) of Arkansas, who proposed that a commission be created by Congress to examine unethical conduct by government officials who accepted gifts and favors in exchange for special treatment for illegals. In his letter he quoted Fulbright's proposal and a report in The New York Times, highlighting one paragraph that said: "The rise in illegal border-crossing by Mexican 'wetbacks' to a current rate of more than 1,000,000 cases a year has been accompanied by a curious relaxation in ethical standards extending all the way from the farmer-exploiters of this contraband labor to the highest levels of the federal government." It was well known that in Eisenhower's time some US immigration officials were social friends of many of the ranchers who hired illegals at very low wages. The officials closed their eyes to the multiple violation of US law. Where was the voice of the church in all of this? Regrettably, it was mute. The New York Times raised the violation of ethical standards, not church officials.

Years later, Eisenhower's first attorney general, Herbert Brownell Jr said that Ike had a sense of urgency about illegal immigration when he became president because there was a full scale breakdown in law enforcement, as "hundreds of thousands were coming in from Mexico [every year] without restraint." Where is Eisenhower now that we need him again, as the number has swelled from three million to a possible twenty million illegals? The United States, the bearer of the torch of freedom, needs to jealously guard the preservation of American sovereignty and America's working class. The report asserts that there are between twelve and fifteen million jobs in the U.S. currently held by illegal aliens, or about 8 percent of the work force.

Immigrant inflows from 2000 to 2005 accounted for 86 percent of the total gain in American employment and approximately two-thirds of these new immigrants are illegal. Among males living in America, illegals make up net growth in employment between those five years. Native-born adults under twenty five are having difficulty finding jobs. Therefore the argument that new immigrants simply take jobs that Americans do not want, is specious. Between four and six million jobs have shifted to the underground economy since 1990. These are not jobs Americans won't do. They are jobs Americans used to do. Areas in the United States that experience less illegal immigration have no problem finding workers for every category of labor. If you travel to the Mountain States and parts of the Midwest you will find that Americans pick the crops, mow the grass, man the quick food restaurants, dig ditches, clean hotel rooms, sell gasoline at the pumps, wash hotel windows, clean our city streets, dispose of our garbage, sell ice cream, work as maids, work at Wallmart, and take care of major and minor construction jobs. Illegals, wherever they go, cause dislocation and economic upheaval. Massive illegal immigration causes as many problems inside Mexico as it does to the United States. The only winners are the Mexican oligarchy and the elite who man corporate America. The United States economy loses about $35 billion a year in income tax collections because of the number of jobs that are now off the books.

Out of Control

Tony Dolz is a national security analyst with the California Coalition for Immigration Reform (CCIR). He is also a founding member of the Minutemen border security and immigration, and the State of California Legislative Liaison for the Minuteman Civil Defense Corps (MCDC). He claims that 3 percent of Illegal Aliens take the lowest of the low paying jobs, but that the remaining 97 percent take Jobs that Americans want and need. The former Wall Street investment firm Bear Stearns published a report, "The Underground Labor Force is Rising to the Surface." The report states that the illegal alien population is double the official government estimates and that the government vastly underestimates the cost of illegal immigration. "When illegal aliens take these jobs they not only take jobs from American teens and drive the wages down but also deny entry level work and the ladder of opportunity from the working poor and legal immigrants – thus making the American Dream harder to obtain." A Pew Hispanic Center poll agrees. It tells us that 97 percent of the two to twenty million illegal aliens are working in construction, hospitality, manufacturing, restaurant, administrative and service jobs, jobs that Americans are happy, even eager to do. They did them from the founding of America until corporate American appetite for profits went totally berserk and thousands of employers opted to break the law by hiring illegal aliens on a grand scale. Steven Malanga notes in "How Unskilled Immigrants Hurt Our Economy," "A handful of industries get low-cost labor, and the taxpayers foot the bill." The Financial Times of May 10, 2005 reported that real wages in the US were falling at their fastest rate in fourteen years.

And, when the present crop of illegal workers becomes legalized, what do politicians do? No problem. Once having secured the illegals amnesty, they move on to another batch of illegals that will also gratefully vote for them if they also get amnesty.

It is time our government stopped bending and/or ignoring its commitment to secure our borders and enforce employer sanctions as promised. Terrorist acts, including the World Trade Center bombing, have underscored the need to keep violent criminals out of the country. Guest Worker programs should be put on the back burner until our borders are secured, employer sanctions are enforced and the last illegal immigrant has left or has been deported from our America. That would be logical and just, not immoral and illogical. After all, in 2006, the immigrant, or foreign-born population, reached about thirty eight million in the United States. Now, legal and illegal immigrants account for one out of every eight persons living in the United States. In 1970 the proportion was one in twenty.

County Sheriff Donald Smith

The following example of law enforcement officials being encouraged not to follow the law by the example of members of Congress and the support of the church is outrageous. In New York State, Putnam County Sheriff Donald Smith said his department would not participate in the federal program known as 287(g), which grants state and local law enforcement the authority to question, arrest and start deportation proceedings against criminal illegal immigrants. The program requires local departments to consult and sign agreements with the U.S. Department of Homeland Security that define the "scope and limitations" of their authority. Officers then participate in a five-week training course to become certified in performing immigration duties under the supervision of ICE. Law enforcement agencies around the nation have signed agreements, with at least four hundred officers trained. The process has paid off with more than 22,000 illegal immigrants arrested, and in 2006 alone, nearly 200,000 illegals were deported overall. .

Brewster, New York, Mayor John Degnan's plan to participate in the federal program, saying it would add another level of expertise to the village's recently revived police force, is popular with the locals. Degnan had no hesitation in proposing the deputizing of village officers to more quickly identify illegal immigrants who are criminals and begin deporting them, especially since the program gives the police department access to national databases to help distinguish between civil and criminal violators. The 287(g) program was created in 1996 to assist federal agents in fighting terrorism and serious crimes. Although it was not designed originally to deal with street crime, its application to murder is most certainly appropriate. Officials of the area had asked Smith to consider the program after several crimes were committed in Brewster involving day laborers, including stabbings and a homicide. His refusal ignited a firestorm, including his own Fraternal Order of Police. Smith had argued that since the department was already working well with Immigration and Customs Enforcement (ICE) and the program would not have a significant impact in Putnam County; he saw no reason to comply. His fellow-citizens could not comprehend why, after several murders had been committed by illegals, the county sheriff did not immediately accept the authority given him to question illegals. He shocked his fellow citizens by making the argument that although he had authority to crack down he would not because he felt it was a Federal, not County issue. A Brewster florist, Mark Buzzetto, said: "The program would benefit. It's a step in the right direction to improve the quality of life in the village of Brewster."

Brewster's Hispanic population was clearly emotionally affected, fearing that their illegal members might be arrested at any moment. However, Hispanic leader, Victor Padilla, tried to allay any fears generated by what the mayor was doing. He agreed that local police should have immigration enforcement powers for criminals.

Sheriff Smith's logic escaped the comprehension of his fellow townsmen. The logic has also escaped everyone else's logical conclusions. Here was the sheriff being handed a critical tool in dealing with the crimes committed, and he refused to use it, something that amazed law enforcement officials around the nation. But, then, the Congress that makes the laws is demanding that Americans ignore the law, so I guess we should not be surprised. And, in addition, leading Christian church leaders are calling for ignoring the law. So, what is a poor sheriff to think? You figure it out.

Chapter Six

The High Cost of Cheap Labor

The chilling cost to our nation of Illegal aliens displacing American workers is enormous, according to Harvard Professor George Borjas. We pay $1.6 billion annually on illegal aliens who rape, murder or sell drugs in this nation, housing, clothing, feeding and entertaining them in our prisons. And the cost of illegal alien anchor babies? More than 300,000 alien women annually arrive pregnant and have their babies in the U.S, thereby forcing the American taxpayer to cover the costs for their education, medical care and a host of other social costs that soar to the hundreds of billions of dollars annually. The granting of citizenship to children of legal or illegal immigrants goes back to 1866. Why does the United States continue to allow a practice subject to widespread abuse? The answer lies in how American courts have interpreted the Fourteenth Amendment to the Constitution. The Fourteenth Amendment was added to the Constitution as part of the post-Civil War reforms aimed at addressing injustices to African-Americans. It states, "All persons born or naturalized in the United States and subject to the jurisdiction thereof are citizens of the United States" and was crafted so that state governments could never deny citizenship to blacks born in the United States.

An estimated one-third to one-half illegal aliens work off the books. California alone pays an average of $79 million to provide emergency medical services for its illegal aliens, resulting in the bankruptcy and closing down, in 2004, of four major hospitals in Los Angeles alone. In 2002, the state of Georgia incurred a $63 million deficit for 64,000 unpaid doctor visits to their Grady Health Care system, and $27 million for 11,188 anchor baby hospital births, plus $242 million for educating illegal alien kids in 2003. Spreadsheet this across the nation and you can see that this nation is bankrupting itself slowly but surely. While all of this is taking place, one in two adult African-Americans in New York is unemployed, and the number of African-American children growing up in poverty increased by 50 percent since 1999 because their adult parents cannot find work.

Our government borrows $1.6 billion daily from foreign banks, as more than 4,000 illegal aliens cross our borders every night to further exacerbate the problem and the costs. The magnitude of the inflow of illegal aliens can be pictured when you realize that enough illegal aliens are pouring into the United States to fill 22,000 737 Boeing airliners at sixty flights every day for a year. And, while our brave troops fight on foreign soil to protect us, their government leaves our borders open for a daily invasion force. Our government officials should not only return all the salaries we pay them, but should also be fined to cover the costs of all those Boeing 737s. To add insult to injury, only twenty-two companies in 2003 were taken to court for hiring illegal aliens and none were incarcerated, even though the legal penalties are $10,000 fines for each illegal alien hired and up to five years in prison. Blatantly breaking the law in this area has no penalty, so we can hardly preach to our youngsters who go to jail for much less. And what about our city and state officials who preach the breaking of the law? Who are they? Well, here is a partial listing: Mayor Bloomberg of New York City, Governor Baldacci of Maine, Governor Bill Owens of Colorado, the mayors of Los Angeles, San Francisco, and Miami. They invoke Special Order 40. Special Order 40 is a policy established in Los Angeles in 1979. It prohibits police officers from "initiating police action with the objective of discovering the alien status of a person." This prevents officers from inquiring about the immigration status of an individual and from contacting federal immigration officials about an individual's immigration status. It violates both federal immigration laws and California law while placing American citizens at risk. While we deploy 150,000 troops to Iraq so that, in the words of then President Bush, "they won't come here," we allow a flood of aliens of all sorts to spill over our borders every day. Make sense? I don't think so. And to make a farce more of a farce, legal immigration is offered only to those who have relatives here, are sponsored by an employer or are seeking political asylum.

The illegal men and women who cut our lawns, dig our ditches, work in sweatshops, mind our children, and work in cattle and chicken slaughterhouses are not the main problem. The employers are the problem. Clearly and unequivocally, the principal agent of cheap labor, and therefore the biggest cause of illegal immigration is the demand of industry for workers who will cost as little as possible. Corporations would probably outsource a lot more unskilled labor jobs than they have already. However, cattle and chicken slaughtering cannot be outsourced by shipping cows from Texas to India, and shipping them back as pot roasts, scented hams and New Delhi-fried chicken.

The Past Was Saner

Some Americans observe that when their forebears migrated to America they did not place great demands on government services. While that would be difficult to prove one way or the other, the fact is that the size of government was significantly smaller at the last great wave of immigration. Expenditures on everything from public schools to roads were only a fraction of what they are today. Thus, the arrival of unskilled immigrants in the past did not have the negative fiscal implications that it does today. The economic profile of America has changed dramatically since the immigration days of our parents and grandparents. However, even in the earliest days, what was deemed to be an excessive number drew the attention of the Congress. In an action designed to keep wages at a level to support a family, The Chinese Exclusion Act became law on May 6, 1882. It cut off Chinese immigration because of low-wage Chinese workers flooding the American labor market.

The Education Factor

The key determinant of economic success today is education. This is why the costs that unskilled immigrants impose on American taxpayers simply reflect the nature of the modern American economy, costs that cannot change if our immigration policies remain unchanged. The demography of households headed by illegal immigrants indicates that illegal alien households have a lower income and are larger in size than the average household in America, primarily due to the fact that most illegals have very little formal education. Perhaps as many as two-thirds of illegals who head families lack a high school diploma, and there is no better predictor of income in the modern American economy than one's education level. During his lifetime an immigrant without a high school education imposes a net fiscal drain on taxpayers of $89,000; for those with only a high school degree it \was $31,000. Aside from those who engage in unlawful activities (and there are many who do) most illegals will remain at or not far from the poverty level, even if they are lucky enough to eventually attain legal status in the country.

Obviously, at that level of financial insecurity, illegals make as wide a use of public services as they possibly can, but not that many receive Social Security or cash welfare programs compared to other households. However, they make liberal use of Medicaid and food assistance welfare programs, far more than do non-illegal households. Most illegals do take advantage of free school lunches or Medicaid services afforded them because they are parents of children born in the United States. The Federal government guarantees food and medical care for these children.

The average illegal household pays roughly one-fifth as much as other households, both because of lower incomes and larger family size. By the very nature of their situation, only half of illegals make payroll contributions. But for more generic and general taxes other than income tax, the difference between illegals and legals is not all that large. They are happy to get a job so the employer does not have to offer them health compensation. The illegal will be very careful not to complain about even the worst conditions because the employer may tell them, "If you can do better somewhere else, go ahead." Also, the illegal will be happy to receive even less than the minimum wage because he knows that there are five hundred others as desperate as he is just waiting for him to say, "I need more money," and then be chosen for the job. All of this game playing on the part of cynical and cruel employers is done in the name of "cheap labor." Fine. We know that corporate American makes a virtue of ruthless bargaining, but we do not have to buy their argument that illegal labor is cheap labor, with one exception, namely that illegal labor is cheap for corporate America. That much is true. However, it is not true for the rest of us. Corporate America's penchant for inviting Americans to enjoy cheap labor is like the man who suggests you go out with him for dinner and then, after the meal, waits for you to pay the bill. Corporate America tells us that goods will be cheaper in the shops because it is using illegal labor. However, it fails to tell you that once you get through with paying the cost of educating, medically treating, and providing municipal services and sufficient jail space for illegals that commit crimes in this country, it is costing you a lot of your hard earned money. In addition, it fails to tell you that thousands of American citizens, especially in the inner city, are suffering the emotional trauma of having loved ones murdered by and traumatized by illegal aliens. If they told you this you would understand that the cost of illegal immigration to our society is incredibly, unbelievably high.

For decades, apart from the immorality of Christians engaging in making money off the blood, sweat, and tears of illegal immigrants, Corporate America shamefully claims that illegal labor is cheap labor. It is not cheap. Since the late 1950s, when illegal laborers began to bring their children and wives and relatives into the country with them, it has become very expensive labor indeed. They may have lived undetected but they began to siphon monies intended for taking care of Americans, as the cost of a wide range of municipal services began to soar. Since there is at any given time just a certain amount of money available for these services it is clear that when illegals in the millions began to share in a given amount of money available, Americans began to suffer. If, as is estimated, the average illegal immigrant has two to four children, the money now needed to provide the added $7000 extra per child puts a great strain, not only on the educational system, but also on the government agencies responsible for providing the funds. When you consider that there are up to or more than twenty million illegals in this nation, you can see that illegal labor is not cheap labor. It is, in fact, very, very expensive labor. The number of students in special English classes is rapidly rising. Between 1995 and 2005, the number of students registered in Limited English Proficiency (LEP) programs increased by more than 1.2 million students (a 38 percent rise), bringing the total number of LEP students to approximately 4.5 million persons. As for schools, although they are primarily paid for by state and local governments, the federal government now provides more than $28 billion for primary and secondary education. Moreover, Washington gives schools assistance in footing the cost of educating children with limited English and for the children of agricultural workers. Illegal households impose very significant costs on the federal education budget because they tend to have more school-age children on average. Since it is estimated that there are about four million children of illegal immigrants in K-12 public school the cost to American taxpayers is enormous. In 2005, approximately 4.5 million K-12 children in our nation's public schools were listed as LEP and required special educational programs to help them master basic English. The burden of funding these programs fell on the American taxpayers to the tune of more than $4 billion a year. And this situation is difficult to overcome because classes and public schooling may not be denied to the children of illegal immigrants under the *Plyler v. Doe* ruling of the Supreme Court in 1982. This ruling is based on an interpretation of the Equal Protection Clause of the Fourteenth Amendment.

The costs for the federal prison and court system are also very high. Illegal aliens account for about 3.6 percent of the nation's total population, but one-fifth of those are in federal prison. The cost to our government is disproportionately high relative to their share of the total population. And, we also have to pay dearly for the cost of forcibly removing the nation's estimated ten million illegal immigrants at $41 billion a year. This is a larger financial burden than the annual budget of the Department of Homeland Security. According to a study: "Deporting the Undocumented: A Cost Assessment," made by the Center for American Progress, arresting, detaining, prosecuting and removing immigrants who have entered the United States illegally or overstayed their visas is a very heavy financial burden indeed. The total cost would be about $220 billion over five years.

Myths

The illegal immigration dilemma gets infested with so much spin and emotion that the use of ordinary language to convey ideas becomes muddled. For example, we need to remember that to call those who cross our borders illegally, "illegal aliens" is not an insulting remark, for it is the only expression that federal laws and regulations use. Another myth is that Mexico is a poor country. In fact, it has the twelfth richest economy in the world, and continues to profit by happily encouraging their less productive citizens to enter the United States. Lou Dobbs, the CNN reporter who, perhaps more than any other media person, provides an accurate analysis of illegal immigration, reported that 33 percent of our prison population is now comprised of non-citizens. Plus, 36 to 42 percent of illegal aliens are on welfare. So, for a good proportion of these people, the American dream is crime and welfare, not coming here to work. .

The current U.S. population is 300 million. The Census Bureau's projection of U.S. population in 2050, based on the legal immigration that occurs in our nation every year, is 420 million. If we add, even modestly, the number of illegal immigrants entering this nation every day of the week, we begin to understand the enormity of the problems that will face our financial system. The total cost of this "subsidized" labor is impossible to ascertain and difficult to even estimate, but it is immense and growing. Cheap labor drives down wages as low income Americans are forced to compete against these admittedly hard working but illegal immigrants. Enormous pressure is placed on employers to "do what every other employer does" by pretending not to know that the men and women whom they hire are undocumented.

Even a cursory reading of newspapers, listening to the radio or watching television on the part of employers guarantees that they know of the industry that produces false documents. Employers pretend not to know about the falsification of documents, and that what they are doing is depressing the wages of American citizens. Their excuse is that if they do not do what others do, they will earn less money and perhaps even have to close their businesses for lack of being able to compete in the marketplace. They are competing with other employers in the race that they know full well is a "race to the bottom," fueled by the sweat and labor of illegal aliens. Professor George Borjas, of Harvard, estimates that American workers lose $190 billion annually in depressed wages caused by the hiring of illegal aliens.

Steven Camarota, director of research at Center for Immigration Studies, is of the opinion that U.S. policy should be to reduce the number of Mexican and low-skill immigrants. He explains that Mexican immigrants, both legal and illegal, are a heavy financial burden on U.S. taxpayers though their use of public assistance. Of course, some argue that we should be accepting of the cost. But, considering that we have so many unmet needs in our nation, from a crumbling physical infrastructure to a lack of widespread insurance guarantees, accepting the cost of subsidizing another nation's population would be like the man who has plenty of money for his mistress, but little for his wife. With reference to labor, he says, "In effect, Mexican immigration acts as a subsidy to businesses that employ unskilled workers, holding down labor costs, while taxpayers pick up the costs of providing services (to them)."

The Visa Lottery

Camarota also addresses the odd visa lottery system. People send in a postcard, and then names are drawn out of a hat, with 50,000 winners each year given permanent residence in the United States. "There are many problems with such a system, but five stand out: 1) it is administratively burdensome; 2) it encourages illegal immigration; 3) it invites fraud; 4) it creates a great opportunity for terrorists; 5) it serves no purpose." Several terrorists arrived in the United States because they won in the lottery, and they have committed acts of terrorism in the United States. Karim Koubriti, from Morocco, was convicted on terrorism-related charges. Ahmed Hannan was acquitted of terrorism charges in the same trial that convicted Koubriti. The most notorious terrorist lottery winner is Hesham Mohamed Hedayet. The forty one year-old Egyptian immigrant limousine driver who, in 2002, shot two people to death and wounded three others at Los Angeles International Airport before being shot to death by security guards..

In addition, the lottery gives a largely false hope to perhaps hundreds of thousand of illegal immigrants that have no hope of acquiring a green card that one day they too may be so lucky. During this waiting period they become more entrenched and more determined to live in this country regardless of circumstances, to the point that should they be ordered to leave one day, the experience of having wasted all that time living with a false hope, having cut precious ties with their family and nation of origin, they have been know to wish to commit suicide rather than return to their own homeland.

These are the most important reasons to stop illegal immigration; they are sufficient to declare illegal immigration into the United States as one of the great immoral acts of our time. Even the best brains in the Congress have come up with midget solutions to this serious problem. They suggest two sets of options. One is to allow illegal aliens to remain in the country, but attempt to reduce the costs they impose. A second set of options would be to grant them legal status as a way of increasing the taxes they pay. First of all, the amount of money that can be saved by curtailing their use of public services even further is probably quite limited because as soon as illegal households receive the benefits granted to their U.S.-citizen children, the cost of their presence skyrockets. As regards increasing tax revenue by granting amnesty, there is widespread agreement among experts that costs would also grow dramatically with legalization. It is estimated that once legalized, payments to illegals under a wide variety of programs would grow more than ten-fold. Legalization will not change the low education levels of illegal aliens or the fact that the American labor market offers very limited opportunities to such workers, whatever their legal status. The fact is that the United States, like all industrialized democracies, has a well-developed and expensive welfare state that provides assistance to low-income workers. So, from a purely fiscal point of view, the main problem with legalization is that illegals would, for the most part, become unskilled legal immigrants. And unskilled legal immigrants create much larger fiscal costs than unskilled illegal aliens. The only real option is to enforce the law and reduce the number of illegal aliens in the country. The centerpiece of enforcement is to enforce the ban on hiring illegal aliens. At present, the law is completely unenforced. Enforcement would require using existing databases to ensure that all new hires are authorized to work in the United States and levying heavy fines on businesses that knowingly employ illegal aliens. Finally, a clear message from policymakers, especially senior members of the administration, that enforcement of the law is valued and vitally important to the nation, would dramatically increase the extremely low morale of those who enforce immigration laws.

The Cost

As of October 7, 2007, below is some of the cost of illegal immigration, according to the very alert Website: ImmigrationCounters.com.

-The numbers of Illegals in the United States may be up to twenty one million, according to a One-

NewsNow.com article by Jim Brown, October 5, 2007. Californians for Population Stabilization estimates, based on a study by former INS legal counsel Jim Walsh, that there are up to thirty eight million illegal immigrants in the U. S. Walsh's analysis uses the conservative estimate of three illegal immigrants entering the U.S. for each one apprehended. According to Walsh, "In the United States, immigration is in a state of anarchy -- not chaos, but anarchy."

-Cost of social services since 1986: $400 billion.

-Number of illegals in public schools: 4 million.

-Cost of illegals in K-12 since 1996: $15 billion.

-Incarcerated Illegal immigrants: 347,802.

-Money wired to Mexico since January. 2006: $72 billion through 2008.

-Money wired to Latin America since 2001: $515 billion through 2008.

-Cost of Incarceration since 2001: $1.5 billion.

-Illegal Immigrant fugitives: 659,696.

-Anchor babies since 2001: more than 2 million

Skilled jobs taken by illegals: more than 10 million

Chapter Seven

Illegal Immigration and Identity Theft

Identity theft and identity fraud refer to any crime that results from the wrongful use of another person's personal data. Unlike fingerprints, which cannot be stolen, your personal records, Social Security Number, bank account or credit card number, telephone calling card number, and other form of ID can be used. By using another person's ID, a thief can raid bank or financial accounts, obtain a federal home loan, a gun or house-trailer, running up enormous bills for his victim. If one receives applications for "preapproved" credit cards in the mail, and tosses them away without first tearing them up, another person can activate the cards and charge articles to them. Also, if your mail is delivered to a place where others have ready access to it, criminals can intercept credit card information. The situation has gotten so out of hand that Congress in 1998 created a new federal offense of identity theft. But, as I mentioned above, even if the government discovers such an offense, in certain areas, they are not allowed either to notify you or do anything about it.

Identity theft is one of the fastest growing crimes in the United States. It is a new crime practiced by counterfeiters, check and credit card forgerers, computer hackers, and impersonators. After its rapid proliferation set off alarm bells among creditors, identity theft became a federal crime in the United States in 1998, when the *Identity Theft Assumption and Deterrence Act.1* was passed. This act identifies offenders as anyone who" knowingly transfers or uses, without lawful authority, any name or number that may be used, alone or in conjunction with any other information, to identify a specific individual with the intent to commit, or to aid or abet, any unlawful activity that constitutes a violation of federal law, or that constitutes a felony under any applicable state or local law."

Identity theft is often practiced by those who repeatedly use a stolen credit card to violate another person's card account, or use stolen personal information to open new accounts. Congressional hearings in the 1990s discovered that police around the nation view the true victims of identity theft as the credit card companies that took the financial loss. Victims, either the real identity owner or the loan companies involved, do not bother to report their losses to law enforcement authorities. The bureaucratic mess involved in even reporting identity theft is so burdensome that victims often accept the fact and go on with their lives. .

The Federal Trade Commission claims that nearly 5 percent of respondents to its 2003 survey admitted that they had been victims of identity theft in the previous twelve months. This amounts to fifteen million victims a year in the United States. The FTC also reported that identity theft is the major subject of consumer complaints—42 percent (214,905) of all those received in 2003. That was up 33 percent from the previous year. Identity theft victims experience long-term harassment and suffering from debt collectors, banks, loan rejection, utility cutoffs, and even arrest for the identity thief's crimes. Perhaps the greatest suffering is the disruption of their lives (an average of six hundred hours trying to sort out the problem) and the psychological damage suffered.

In 2005, identity theft complaints made up 37 percent of all fraud complaints in the United States. The information revolution that has transformed the lives of students, businessmen and the various communications media has also increased opportunities for criminal activity. Crimes units all over the nation receive reports about identity thieves and con artists every day.

Added to the List of Immoral Acts

In 2001, Social Security reports show that as much as 35 percent of the wages in its earnings suspense fund were earned by workers in California. This sets off alarms that 35 percent, a large proportion of the funds, come from illegal aliens working in agriculture. Other indications include the illegal aliens finding employment in restaurants and similar service industries. It is also important to note that lost or stolen wallets, checkbooks or credit cards are the primary source of personal information theft. So, be extra careful. The thirty-five to forty-five demographic age group has the highest traditional types of fraud. The average fraud for this group amounts to $9,435. For the technically competent it can be noted that electronic account monitoring is the fastest way to detect fraud and leads to lower losses - (twenty two days to become aware of the theft and $3,806 theft).

Those who gain from these crimes include: The IRS and Social Security (they collect extra taxes), loan agencies have more customers, and corporate America adds more cheap labor to its list of employees. .

Problem Magnified

The problem of identity theft was magnified by a federal requirement put in place in 1986, that workers were obliged to present Social Security cards when applying for work. By creating a black market for counterfeit Social Security cards, the law kicked off the identity theft crisis, and this did not include the uncounted numbers still hidden. Since the Immigration Reform and Control Act of 1986, workers must produce a Social Security card or similar identity verification when obtaining employment. Employers are supposed to verify that the card is legitimate, but many don't. By creating a black market for counterfeit Social Security cards, the law may have inadvertently kicked off the identity theft crisis, experts say. "It's truly an unintended consequence of the 1986 immigration law," said Marilanne Hincapie of the National Immigration Law Center. In the year 2002 nine million hard working Americans were defrauded. This is in one year alone!! Each year millions of FICA payments sent to the government as Social Security funds contain inaccurate, highjacked names and numbers.

The Earnings Suspense File

The amount of unaccredited Social Security wages is now an enormous $420 billion, an amount that sits in what's called the Earnings Suspense File, an accounting limbo. The Social Security Administration, having no knowledge of the correct sender, just sits on all that money, money that could be used, for example, to buttress the ailing Social Security system. The amount of money headed for the Earnings Suspense File began to skyrocket after 1986, when a new federal law required workers to produce Social Security cards to get employment. In 2002, about 46 percent of the wages that ended up in the fund come from immigrant-heavy industries like agriculture, restaurants and other services, according to Social Security's Office of Inspector General. Both facts suggest to analysts that much of the fund is the result of payments made by undocumented immigrant workers. Just how many of those millions of payments were made by illegal aliens using other persons Social Security numbers is not clear. However, an educated guess would easily suggest that several hundred thousand identity thefts were involved. One would think that if the government really wanted to locate illegal aliens, an investigation of what illegal alien holds which of the duplicated Social Security Numbers would be rigorously pursued. However, the Social Security Administration says that to disclose that information would be breaking the law! No, I'm not kidding. Let me put it another way. For a Social Security official to reveal which illegal alien is both violating the law of illegal entry and committing an act of fraud, is against federal Law.

You can't believe this? Believe it. And try this. If you discover some odd things going on in your life, like getting billed twice for your car payments and you ask the government if someone else is using your Social Security Number, they will not tell you. Neither does the government allow itself to notify to you if an illegal alien has filed a return using your Social Security Number In another major blow to rational enforcement, the Supreme Court in May, 2009, ruled in *Flores-Figueroa v. United States* that persons taking another person's Social Security Number cannot be charged with the crime of identity theft unless they *know* that they have stolen it from another person. Welcome to the decline of the Roman Empire!

The Internet

Not surprisingly, identity thieves have gone global by acquiring information on the internet. A password can be stolen. While working in Trinidad, I was forced to change my password frequently after a local internet company employee informed me that the reason I kept getting busy signals attempting to get on line was because someone had stolen my password and was freely using it. He even went so far as to say that it was most likely an employee of the Internet Service, since they had ways of stealing passwords. He suggested that I change my password weekly. It was a nuisance, but I did it. And then there is the appealing mail that promises great benefits to those who supply their passwords or banking information, assuring the reader that such information will be kept strictly confidential. With a stolen ID, a criminal can commit a wide range of crimes, including false applications for loans and credit cards, fraudulent withdrawals from bank accounts, and fraudulent use of telephone calling cards. It is simple for a criminal to have the bills for the falsely obtained goods sent to an address other than the victim's. Thus, by the time the victim is notified of his "debts" and warnings are sent to him about failure to make payments, the criminal may already have inflicted substantial damage on the victim's credit and reputation. Neither the Internal Revenue Service nor the Social Security Administration has ever released the number of such defrauders, but there are some solid hints suggesting that hundreds of thousands of people are currently at risk of "lending" their identity to an illegal alien. Most consumers only discover the situation when their defrauders secure credit using the stolen number. And even then, the victims may not discover this until the thief misses a loan payment. Credit obtained by imposters using their real name but a stolen Social Security number does not appear

CONTENTS

on the victim's credit report. Instead, the credit bureaus create "subfiles," which, in effect, are separate identities. Payments made by workers that landed in the Earnings Suspense File, as of 2002, amounted to $56 billion. You wonder what in the name of heaven is going on in our government when the IRS, which is supposed to fine a business that does not collect the social security number information of defrauders, never does. Is this a bureaucratic nightmare or what? A businessman can pay a fee to see any transactions tied to your social security number, but you cannot. One would suspect that a major conspiracy is taking place involving the entire top tier of government but, after reflection, when you observe their actions, you end up concluding that they are not intelligent enough for that.

You might discover one day that someone has used your Bank of America credit card because you have naively disclosed your credit card number on the internet to what you presume is a legitimate business. The e-mailer assures you that the company's security measures will protect you from account thieves or any other fraudulent actions. In such cases, even if the owner of the e-mail who tricked you is discovered, he can get away with his scam. He simply claims that someone else must have used his e-mail address to do this dastardly act. He simply promises to change his e-mail ID and password so that no one can do this in the future. He then changes his ID and password and continues defrauding others. A Chicago man charged with making fake identification for illegal immigrants plea-bargained after he was caught. He assisted the police in arresting eight people. The man was Joseph M. Kalady, sixty one. His business was making fake birth certificates that were used to obtain Social Security cards and passports. His fee was $5,000. At that rate, the selling of ten false documents would give him a comfortable yearly salary, but it is more likely he sold ten a week. .

What Can You Do?

If you discover that someone is using your identity at your expense, and the government is lazily sipping mint tulips while your life is being disrupted, what can you do? There is one thing you can do. You can contact the fraud departments of the three major credit bureaus, and request that your file be tagged with a "fraud alert tag." That will not eliminate your problem, but it will make it more difficult for a thief because any new creditors will notify you before granting credit. You can ask that creditors call you before granting credit for a period of seven years.

Information on Credit Bureaus

CardCops monitors internet chat rooms and other hacker communications for stolen credit card numbers, and then notifies merchants and consumers to block bad purchases. It is possible, but possibly illegal, to log into a defrauder's account and find yourself a treasure trove of stolen financial information and even the identity of the defrauder. The law in these matters is so complex and so ridiculous that you are not allowed to play detective to protect yourself.

The stories of police agencies being very reluctant to go after these crooks are legendary. For example, if a Canadian defrauds you and you report this to the police, you might well be told that: "The Canadian police will have to help you." The likelihood of that happening is not very good. For example, the Royal Canadian Mounted Police in Quebec do not investigate online financial crimes, and city police refer such cases to provincial police, a route that takes months to get started. In other words, online defrauders carry on their criminal activity with impunity. They make a mess of a hardworking American's work history, Social Security benefits records and credit reports. Victims are haunted by bills and creditors. They receive threatening letters from the IRS, asking them to pay taxes on money earned by the defrauders. The Social Security Administration has made some efforts to straighten out its records. In 2002, the agency sent 900,000 letters to companies that had workers using erroneous names or numbers. Immigration rights groups objected, pointing out that inclusion in a no-match list was not an automatic indicator of illegal status, so the SSA effort was in vain. Is this not some sort of total insanity? Here is a Rights group arguing that the no-match list would violate the rights of illegals, who have no citizen rights, and not a word about the violation of the hundreds of thousands of citizens who do have citizen rights.

Meanwhile, the IRS, which is charged with enforcing the requirement that employers collect accurate Social Security number data, has never once levied a fine against a corporation for failing to do so. One suggestion I have is that the government, since it does not want to investigate thieves for fear of violating their civil rights, could get off the hook by teaching the public how to defraud the defrauders. They can then close their eyes and allow the good guys to catch the bad guys.

Federal law requires that each of the three credit bureaus provide one free credit report per year to an individual upon request. This you can order at each of the three bureaus at the Annual Credit Report Web site. A tiny bit of good news. The number of adult victims of identity fraud in the United States declined marginally between 2003 and 2006, from 10.1 million people to 8.9 million people. However, victims are spending more time working their way out of fraud-induced difficulties. The time spent increased from thirty-three hours in 2003 to forty hours in 2006. It is important to note that people are not totally helpless in protecting themselves from identity theft but, the swifter the reporting to authorities takes place the less the loss. For example, if a victim is quick to report, he or she is not likely to bear the brunt of financial losses from identity fraud; it is also a comforting thought that seniors are not the most frequent targets of identity thieves.

During 2002, the most recent figures available, nine million people paid taxes with mismatched names and Social Security numbers. Included in that number were women who had failed to notify the agency that their name changed after marriage.

Some were the result of poor typing. But most were the result of illegal immigrants using stolen Social Security numbers at the workplace. Even if this information is checked against the data at a national credit-rating service, the lender will encounter no concerns, as all of the victim's information matches the records. The lender has no easy way to discover that the thief is pretending to be the victim, especially if an original, government-issued ID can't be verified. This is the case when correspondence takes place online, by mail, telephone, and fax. The criminal has the money in his pocket, the lender is never repaid, and the victim is falsely accused of defaulting on a loan he or she took out. This so-called "SSN-only" identity theft poses a unique set of problems for consumers and the nation's credit bureaus. If a lender grants credit, an entry is made in credit bureau files, but not disclosed to the consumer who properly owns that number. Even when a consumer gets a copy of his/her credit report, such fraudulent accounts don't appear on the report. Instead, the credit bureaus create what are sometimes called "subfiles." They become secret identities filed away.

Earnings Suspense File Skyrockets

The amount of money headed for the Earnings Suspense File began to skyrocket after 1986, when a new federal law required workers to produce Social Security cards to get employment. James Huse Jr., former inspector general of the Social Security Administration, said it is unlikely the agency will ever inform potential victims."(The list) would be a terrific source of leads for the identity remediation effort, but there are so many other compelling workloads in front of (SSA) I don't know what they can do with that today," he said. "Also, the politics of immigration get involved in this." A spokesman for the Social Security Administration said the agency simply couldn't disclose the information to consumers because doing so would run afoul of federal law.

Since the estimated number of illegals may top twenty million, a large number of Social Security numbers and driver's licenses are needed. One way to get these documents fraudulently is to read the obituaries and birth announcements to obtain the name and birth date of a person, in order to obtain a birth certificate. With your identity information it is also not difficult to forge or obtain a valid replacement Social Security card. Oftentimes children are targeted because use of their Social Security numbers can go undetected for up to eighteen years. This makes applying for a student loan or looking to purchase a vehicle relatively easy. In one state the authorities searched and matched their records of children receiving welfare with a database of workers paying local and state taxes. There were 1,800 minor victims. Some victims apply for work, let us say at Target, only to find that they already work there-at least Social Security numbers already work there. In one case the same Social Security number had been used to obtain work at thirty-seven other workplaces.

The national average times a single Social Security number is used is thirty times. MSNBC.com claims that hundreds of thousands of Americans have been defrauded in this way. These victims only discover the rip off when they are called upon to pay back taxes or loans obtained by the persons carrying their identities. The amazing thing is that there is no government aggressive task force assigned to do anything about these crimes. Can you check to see if someone is using your Social Security number in this manner? Of course not. Employers and the church see to that by "persuading" politicians in Congress to turn a blind eye to the problem. You will only find out there is a problem. For example, if the person who stole your ID misses a loan payment. Victims can have trouble getting disability or unemployment benefits, or the IRS might be demanding payment of back taxes for wages earned by those who stole the victim's identity, their imposters. The garnishing of a victim's wages can also take place. Why? Because credit obtained fraudulently doesn't appear on the victim's credit report.

IRS Does Not Check

You will not believe this, but according to IRS spokesman Anthony Burke, the agency doesn't check for number-name mismatches until it processes tax returns. And it does not have a mechanism for informing the rightful Social Security number holder that someone else has filed a return using that number. When tax returns are filed with wrong Social Security numbers the agency simply notifies the filer in writing. The rightful number holder isn't told. How can a consumer unravel the secret life of his or her Social Security number? In fact, since neither the government nor private industry is speaking out, there is no way. Asking the Social Security Administration or IRS won't help. Most consumers only discover the situation when their imposters take the next step up the economic ladder, securing credit using the stolen number. And even then, the victims may not be told unless the imposter misses a loan payment or otherwise sends creditors hunting for their money. That's because thanks to a quirk in the credit system, credit obtained by imposters using their real name but a stolen Social Security number doesn't appear on the victim's credit report!

If an imposter is using a consumer's Social Security number but his own name and address is known, a consumer-disclosed credit report won't include that information, so the rightful number holder remains in the dark. Businesses interested in giving credit to a consumer can pay to see any activity connected to a particular Social Security number; consumers cannot. Companies that have signed agreements with credit bureaus can access data, but the credit bureau can't allow consumers to have access. The credit bureau could run into legal trouble for exposing information about a defrauder. "This is the schizophrenia of the federal government," Huse, the former Social Security inspector general said. "The Homeland Security people are screaming about the accuracy of records, and you have the IRS taking money from wherever it comes."

IRS Does not Notify Those Defrauded!

Marti Dinerstein, president of Immigration Matters, a public-policy analysis firm in New York said: "This is total purgatory that this puts U.S. citizen taxpayers into. It's a nightmare to get it stopped. And when they do get it stopped, it is only for that particular year. The whole mess could begin anew next tax season." In the meantime, neither the Social Security Administration nor the IRS has any public plans to attempt to notify consumers who might be sharing an identity with one undocumented worker, or even twenty. Betsy Broder, the attorney in charge of the Federal Trade Commission's efforts to combat identity theft, sympathizes with the challenge facing the IRS and SSA. "Of course consumers are always better off if they know how their information is being misused. But having said that, it's really complex with federal agencies," she said. "There are restrictions under the Privacy Act. You can't release to one person another person's information. And the agencies are often not in a position to know with any certainty who was the right person and who the imposter was"

From an early September, 2007 edition of the South Bend Tribune we learn that a man who was indicted (under seventeen names) with making and possessing false identification cards made his initial appearance in federal court in Hammond, Indiana. He had so many names that he had to be indicted on one of his false names, i.e. Juan Medina, one of his aliases. He was charged in thirteen counts with unlawfully producing false identification documents, possession with intent to transfer such documents, possessing equipment to make the false documents and misuse of a Social Security number. He had in his possession false Illinois identification cards, false Social Security cards, a false El Salvadoran identification card, false driver's licenses, false Mexican identification cards, false U.S. permanent residence cards and the equipment to make them. The government sought an order to forfeit to the United States the false documents and equipment, including a computer system, card printers, a typewriter and blank white plastic cards used to make the false IDs.

The amount of crimes committed because of the illegal alien issue should make anyone, churchman or layman, realize that supporting such activity is immoral, period, whether it is preached by a high ranking churchman or a street vendor. Although it is more likely preached by a high-ranking churchman than a street vendor, because the street vendor is conscious of what is going on in the street.

Sympathy is admirable, but is our culture so paralyzed that it cannot fix the darn problem? Here is where the prophetic voice of the church should be heard. To repeat, we already have more than a million legal immigrants entering the United States each year. Help them. Do not put a stamp of approval on illegal entry, identity theft, rape and mayhem on the part of illegal immigrant criminals from around the world. History will be scandalized by the role the Christian church has played in illegal immigration.

Chapter Eight

Children of Illegal Immigrants: Their Condition

The United States has traditionally accepted immigrants and refugees from around the world. Ordinarily, persons desiring such status apply for entry while residing in their own countries or in a third country known as a "country of first asylum." However, minors unaccompanied by adult relatives have been entering the United States since 1978 without any prior administrative processing. Most of these minors, with the cooperation of their relatives, entered or attempted to enter the United States in violation of law.

The Child Relief Service (CRS) has provided temporary shelter care and other related services to unaccompanied minors apprehended and detained by the INS in South Florida and Texas. They are provided physical care and maintenance while they undergo Citizenship and Immigration Service (CIS) proceedings. Since 1987, significant numbers of minors have crossed our borders, especially those of Texas and California. Many of them make their way to Mexico from El Salvador, Nicaragua, Guatemala, and Honduras. Since 1991, there have been increasing numbers of alien minors apprehended at airports and on both coasts of the United States. When apprehended by federal authorities, the minors are taken to a CIS district office or border patrol office. The CIS requires that minors be released or transferred to an appropriate childcare facility within seventy-two hours of apprehension. Many of them (primarily males fifteen to seventeen years of age) are heading for parents, other relatives, godparents, or friends already residing in the United States. Females comprise approximately 15 percent of the total population of alien minors. For the most part these children are found to be without behavioral or psychological problems. Although placed in the physical custody of the CRS, they remain in the legal custody of the CIS. It takes a good deal of administrative expertise to manage the intricate and complex needs of these children in order to live up to the standards of United States law. This delicate work continues non-stop from the time when the minor is placed in the Shelter Care Program to the time that the child is released by CIS, transferred to another facility, or deported from the United States.

The primary focus is on teenagers but there are many instances of having to take care of children twelve years of age and younger. The services include access to routine and emergency medical care, education, recreation, individual and group counseling, access to religious services, and reunification efforts. Children are tracked and monitored on a regular basis to see to it that each child receives a fully integrated and comprehensive range of program services. All programs must be licensed under the respective state laws. Services must be rendered without restraining construction typically associated with correctional facilities, while at the same time not encouraging and allowing in any shape or form, runaways. At all times, those in whose care the children are assigned are urged to be respectful of the illegals' language, customs and ethnicity. Some of these children are actually illiterate in their own languages and are in need of instruction. Often, the services provided for these children take place in a residential, foster, or group care setting program. Since the children may either arrive at any hour or need to leave at any hour, the service providers work on a twenty-four hour per day, seven days a week basis. The highly structured program of activities is designed to neutralize anti-social behavior.

The daily routine consists of education, recreation, vocational experiences or chores, study period, counseling, group interaction, free time, and access to religious and legal services. Minors are often in and out of the program in thirty days or less. They are given a wide range of rights, such as private space, private telephone conversations and visits, as well as access to legal counsel and religious services of their choice. It does appear that the program works well, but precise information on the number of unaccompanied children populating these centers and programs and their ultimate disposition is not easily available.

On the one hand it is not easy for the United States to ignore the moral dilemma of children as young as five to ten years old purposely being placed over the border as pawns in the game of entering the U.S. for a future advantage for the parents and guardians. On the other hand we need to reverse the anarchic immigration policy that forces the dilemma upon us in the first place. It is simply a reflection of the government's unconscionable abetting of the entire illegal immigration phenomenon; it smacks of government participation in human smuggling operations. One can only assume that those involved in child smuggling consider the U. S government as their greatest friend and co-conspirator, as it blinks, nods and ignores the introduction of children into sweatshop labor or sexual servitude. It seems to me that technically this entire government bureaucracy contains dozens and dozens of immigration officials, and their administrative and congressional colleagues, who deserve jail time.

The United States Senate

Late on the evening of December 21, 2005 the U.S. Senate unanimously passed the Unaccompanied Alien Child Protection Act of 2005 (S.119) introduced by Sen. Diane Feinstein (D-CA). The bill sought to establish minimum standards for the care of unaccompanied alien children who are in federal government custody, including mechanisms that would ensure that all such children have access to counsel as they navigate the complexities of U.S. immigration law. Senator Feinstein re-introduced her bill in spring 2007 during Senate debate on comprehensive immigration reform. This bill (S.844 in the 110th Congress) included the following critical due process protections:

-States that the Office of Refugee Resettlement (ORR) should ensure that all unaccompanied minors in ORR custody should have competent immigration counsel.

-Requires the Department of Justice to develop and implement model guidelines for legal representation of such children.

-Bars children from accepting removal orders or voluntary departure unless the child has had the opportunity to consult with counsel first.

-Authorizes ORR to appoint qualified and trained advocates for immigrant children.

Definition

An alien minor is defined as a male or female foreign national less than eighteen years of age who is detained in the custody of CIS and is the subject of exclusion or deportation proceedings under the Immigration and Nationality Act (INA). Many alien minors, when apprehended by the CIS, are not accompanied by a family member, such as a parent, grandparent, adult sibling, aunt or uncle. They come for a variety of reasons. Some are seeking work, others running away from sex exploitation, bonded labor, or female genital mutilation. Others are abandoned children, runaways, and victims of trafficking of various forms, including sexual exploitation. These children are here, illegally, often alone, exposed to all sorts of dangers, and facing the U.S. legal system alone. U.S. immigration law and policy have consistently failed to meet the special needs of these children. Of the five thousand or so children that have annually been taken into custody, many have remained for an indefinite period in detention facilities here in the United States. They do experience, in some cases, shackling and strip searches, and have even been held with violent juvenile offenders.

Previously, the children came under the jurisdiction of the CIS, which served as both the children's jailer and the party entrusted with determining the children's U.S. immigration status. For a variety of reasons, the CIS methodology was not considered competent in meeting the special needs of these children. So, The Homeland Security Act of 2002 transferred responsibility for the care and placement of these children from INS to the Department of Health and Human Services (DHHS), Office of Refugee Resettlement (ORR). This transfer of responsibility marks an important change in U.S. treatment of unaccompanied alien minors, in that the best interests of such children will now be determined by an agency that has extensive experience in the welfare and immigration needs of children. This change became effective on March 1, 2003. Notwithstanding this transfer of responsibility, the legal terrain has changed very little for unaccompanied alien minors.

From an immigration law perspective, these children face all the legal limitations that adult foreign nationals do. The United States Supreme Court has long recognized that most constitutional provisions are applicable to non-citizens, even those who illegally enter the United States. In *Shaughnessy v. United States*, the court ruled that aliens are entitled to due process before being deported: "Aliens who have once passed through our gates, even illegally, may be expelled only after proceedings conforming to traditional standards of fairness encompassed in due process of law." The Court has assured such persons that they enjoy guaranteed due process of law by the Fifth and Fourteenth Amendments. In some ways, because of their vulnerability, this is especially true of children.

However, although in theory non-citizens have a right to an attorney, there is no obligation on the part of the government to pay for such a service and few aliens can afford such costs. Therefore very few undocumented children have representation in legal proceedings against them. And since deportation itself is not a punishment, no Eighth Amendment protections against cruel or unusual punishment can be asserted. Rules of evidence do not generally apply in deportation proceedings, nor are Miranda warnings required to be given to detained undocumented people. In fact, even Fourth Amendment rights are not generally applicable, and evidence obtained in what would otherwise constitute illegal searches or seizures can still be admissible in removal proceedings. Likewise, no Fifth Amendment right to remain silent applies, so remaining silent is not an option. In practice, it turned out that, under INS detention, unaccompanied children were often intimidated into making admissions that made them deportable. The 1985 *Flores v. Reno* settlement agreement continues to govern the custodial care and treatment of unaccompanied immigrant minors in the United States. The agreement requires the government to place children for whom release is pending or for whom no release option is available in the least restrictive setting appropriate to the child's age and special needs. But, there are exceptions to the rule.

Shelter and Care for Unaccompanied Alien Children

In 1987, the United States Department of Justice (DOJ), Community Relations Service (CRS), and the Immigration and Naturalization Service (INS) (when it had responsibility for alien children) entered into an agreement to establish a network of community based shelter care programs to provide physical care and maintenance and other child welfare related services to alien minors detained in the custody of the CIS. This program (UAC) aims to provide an appropriate environment for unaccompanied alien children from the time they are discovered until they are released from custody by the Office of Refugee Resettlement (ORR), or removal from the United States by the Department of Homeland Security. This program is not perfect but it is the opinion of most observers that it does adequately fulfill its mission. Suggested improvements are more accountability, and more sophisticated management, given the fact that the growing number of children who are apprehended and referred for placement increased by 26 percent in fiscal year 2005; remained relatively stable in fiscal year 2006; and is expected to experience annual increases of approximately 20 percent in future years. For this reason, it would definitely improve the already adequate situation if regular and long term independent evaluations were permitted, because at the present time the program does not show evidence of improved efficiencies or cost effectiveness. However, I must credit those who are working in the program as dedicated and hardworking. Better management seems to be the key to improvement.

Children in federal custody still have no guarantee of legal counsel and no guarantee of the appointment of "guardian at law." (The person appointed by the court to look out for the best interests of the child during the course of legal proceedings.) There is also a lack of bed spaces in appropriate settings to ensure that the children are not mixed with juvenile delinquents. While the former Immigration and Naturalization Service (INS – now CIS) was responsible for the care of the children they used dental radiograph exams to determine the age of unaccompanied children. This test was not totally reliable and resulted in many juveniles being misclassified as adults. Being detained in adult quarters was not conducive to enhancing the condition of minors.

Legal Remedies for Child Victims of Trafficking

Children are eligible for the same immigration assistance as adults. One legal remedy available to child victims of trafficking is Special Immigrant Juvenile Status, a remedy that dates back 1990 when Congress provided legal immigration status that includes the phrase "best interests of the child" to children who become juvenile court dependents. It covers care for non-U.S. citizen minors who have been victims of abuse, neglect, or abandonment. The Special Immigrant Juvenile Status covers these children. Eligibility for this status requires that the child must be physically present in the United States, declared dependent on a juvenile court, and certified by the court as one who, for reasons of the child's best interests, should not be returned to his or her home country. There were management problems with implementation of these safeguards during the period of time that the INS had responsibility for the Children. But now that the authority lies in the hands of the Office of Refugee Resettlement (ORR), much management progress has been made. This is especially consoling because child victims of human trafficking have far more problems and face even greater legal obstacles than other unaccompanied alien minors. Their medical and psychological needs are much greater. It is obvious that these children are particularly vulnerable victims of trafficking and anyone who is working with child victims needs the assistance of highly trained and skilled interview specialists.

Rights of Children in General

As I said above, in the United States children have the same basic right to constitutional protection as adults. But, when child illegals reach the United States with little money and limited ability to speak or understand English, they are at a distinct disadvantage. Some manage to reach migrant labor communities or locate relatives already living in American cities, and they merge unnoticed into the American population, often becoming legal permanent residents in time. But in1990, for example, 8,500 of them were arrested, 70 percent of whom were unaccompanied by an adult guardian. They needed protection and slowly but surely they got it. In 1979, the court reaffirmed the principle established in the 1967 in re Gault case: "Neither the Fourteenth Amendment nor the Bill of Rights is for adults only." In *Bellotti,* the Supreme Court was careful to point out that in addition to their basic constitutional rights, children may even require additional legal protection: As Mr. Justice Frankfurter aptly put it: "Children have a very special place in life which law should reflect.. . . ..Constitutional principles [must] be applied with sensitivity and flexibility to the special needs of parents and children." In *Perez-Funez v. INS,* (1984) for instance, a federal trial court in California found that the INS had violated the due process rights of unaccompanied minors by forcing them to accept voluntary departure from the United States (thus waiving their right to a hearing before an immigration judge) without their effective knowledge or consent.

Responsibility Shift

On March 1, 2003 the care and placement of UAC (Unaccompanied Alien Children) was transferred from the Commissioner of the Immigration and Naturalization Service to the Director of the Office of Refugee Resettlement. The ORR is now responsible for making and implementing placement decisions for the UAC, ensuring that the child's interests are dominant in any decisions related to his/her care and custody.

Shelters for UAC

Unaccompanied alien children are generally provided a method, legal or illegal, of leaving their homes in order to reunite with family already residing, legally or illegally, in the United States, but that is not the only reason. Sometimes they leave for the US to escape physical and/or psychological abuse. If they are old enough to work, they often leave to earn money for supporting their families in the home country. Over a number of years the number of children in ORR care averaged approximately 1,000 per year. In recent times at least, the largest percentage of unaccompanied alien children have come from El Salvador (in 2006 it stood at 32 percent), followed by Honduras and Guatemala. The children are cared for in a total (minimum) of forty ORR-funded facilities in ten different states, usually located adjacent to areas where immigration officials apprehend large numbers of these children. The facilities include classroom education, health care, socialization/recreation, vocational training, mental health services, family reunification, access to legal services, and case management. Most of the children are placed in shelters and group homes. However, in the case of a child who has a documented criminal history, or who exhibits strange or unusual behavior, more secure placement options are available. Some of the more difficult cases are when the child has no evident sponsor to be with him/her while he or she goes through the system. This can be a temporary need. Long-term foster care is also made available during immigration proceedings, and long-term foster care is available through the Office of Refugee Resettlement (ORR) foster care program network

Attorney Needs

Pro-bono attorney outreach is provided to assist children in resolving any legal problems and complications that arise. One area that needs close legal observation is always the potential for trafficking among the unaccompanied alien children. Agencies that may become involved in making judgments about the placing of children include the Department of Homeland Security, CIS, Customs and Border Patrol, the Department of Justice, Executive Office for Immigration Review (EOIR), and non-profit community-based legal service providers. ORR is also responsible for identification and release policy for "unaccompanied minors" caught trying to cross the border or caught in the interior of the United States. ORR is a social services agency that dispenses grant money and manages benefits and services for a wide range of entitled immigrants that now extends well beyond those who come over on the U.S. refugee program. Its clients are eligible for all forms of welfare but, as well, there is grant money from a large number of federal programs to assist a variety of immigrant cases, including the unaccompanied alien child. And, lots of money and legal assistance is needed, because about 100,000 illegal aliens under the age of eighteen are stopped at the border each year. Most of these are Mexicans traveling with relatives or other adults and are simply sent back with a "voluntary departure" status when they are caught with nabbed illegal immigrants. This return status means they may attempt to enter again and again without penalty. ORR contracts out shelters to agencies such as the U.S. Conference of Catholic Bishops and Lutheran Immigration Services. As many as 850 children can be in such shelters on a given day. Most minors who are stopped and taken into custody at the border are joining relatives who arrived earlier. In many cases minors are caught with parents or other adult relatives who are placed in deportation proceedings with DHS, while the minor is placed in the custody of ORR. In these cases, the child, perhaps coached by lawyers and his social network in the United States, can remain in the country even if his parent is deported and wishes for his child to go with him. According to border patrol agents, even minors with head-to-toe MS-13 gang tattoos are handed over to ORR for eventual release to individuals who are also illegally in the country. Gang affiliation is no bar to entry. Many, if not most, get to the border with the help of a smuggler. If caught, the unaccompanied child essentially waits until picked up by a relative in a shelter like Boys Town in Miami or Southwest Key in El Paso and San Diego. These shelters are practically off-limits to DHS agents. Smugglers stopped at the border with children of all ages—even toddlers—know their charges will be conducted safely to the individual who summoned them. If the wait in custody is projected to exceed three months, the minor goes into short-term foster care.

Improving Conditions

That there is continuous need for reforms was reflected in the actions of the 108th Congress, when Sen. Feinstein and Rep. Zoe Lofgren proposed further reforms beyond those passed in the Homeland Security Act. The bill passed the Senate unanimously, but stalled in the House. In the 109th Congress, the proposed reform again would provide structure for pro bono counsel so children do not have to navigate the judicial system alone, and it would allow the appointment of guardians *ad litem*, adults trained in child welfare. It would ensure that unaccompanied children are housed in shelters or in foster care if their own families are unable to care for them. For situations when detention is absolutely necessary, the bill would establish minimum standards of care.

Arizona: A Case Study in the Need for Reform

Arizona has an unaccompanied immigrant child shelter bed capacity of 131, which includes short-term foster care and a secure setting. Currently only one full-time attorney, who is employed by LIRS (Lutheran Immigration and Refugee Service) is available to provide pro bono representation for these children. The Florence Immigrant and Refugee Rights (FRRP) Project is also a nonprofit legal service organization that provides free legal services to men, women and children detained by Immigration and Customs Enforcement. With such a large caseload, it is impossible to provide sufficient legal counsel to each child. An attorney trying to discern a child's legal options needs to build a trusting relationship with the child. This takes time, especially for a child who is fearful of returning to an abusive parent or situation. But an attorney with such a large caseload doesn't have the luxury of spending numerous meetings with each child. The pro bono attorney in Arizona can't even appear in court with every child, so some must go to court alone even though the Department of Homeland Security always sends an attorney to court to push for the removal of the child.

Generally, individuals receiving the unaccompanied child must show kinship, but pre-arranging for a "relative" to step forward and claim sponsorship is the least of a smuggler's concerns. Cousins and great aunts have been used for this purpose. Relationship and the suitability of the sponsor are crucial. Is the person claiming relationship really a relative? Is the child being handed over to a smuggler who will then demand ransom from relatives? Is the child being handed over to be someone's domestic servant?

Is the relative here legally? Unfortunately, the last question is not considered by ORR. Some at the Department of Homeland Security describe a reigning "believe the children" mentality at ORR, which leads to ill-considered and hasty release of minors before these questions can be answered satisfactorily.

Summer Camp.

ORR boasts that it has doubled the release rate of the old INS for minors and greatly improved conditions for them while in federal custody. ORR coordinates with legal services providers for help establishing immigration status, contracts out psychological counseling services for troubled UACs, and contracts to shelter providers, which are more like summer camps than detention centers. In fact, the UAC's stay in shelter care is something of a teenage idyll, with movies every night at some facilities, one counselor per six children, and even horseback riding at one camp. The Office of Refugee Resettlement (ORR) requires that its contractors "maintain a written plan and periodic schedule for exposure to and participation in appropriate cultural events" calculated to ensure the "preservation of ethnic and religious heritage." There have been a few cases where UACs, referred to as "clients" by shelter staff, simply walk out of the unsecured shelter never to be seen again. Client escape statistics are not kept. ORR's goal is to release the minor within a month, but it often releases minors within two weeks. Only if there is a known record of a violent crime or if the youth exhibits particularly violent behavior does the UAC enter a secure detention facility. (Disruptive behavior while in custody seems to only warrant counseling sessions.) Some crimes would not pose an obstacle to entry for an Unaccompanied Alien Child (UAC) or even a guarantee that the UAC will be housed in a secure facility. ORR seldom has access to criminal records from Central American countries, given the short time frame and the fake identities used by many smuggled entrants. In fact, ORR has no expertise in background research and identity fraud and little institutional interest in pursuing it under its "best interest of the child" mandate. This is an area that needs improvement. For the sake of all these children, we need to keep an eye on this.

Chapter Nine

Illegal Immigration and National Security

Immigration has most certainly played a major role in American history, a role that is unique among the nations of the world. Our government has demonstrated a generous willingness to assimilate outsiders. In fact, it is this nation's trademark. But, we know from experience that we have had our share of terrorists crossing our borders. Jacobins, communists, and fascists came to the United States to preach their doctrines with the expectation of getting political and financial support. However, we are now facing a different terrorist; the terrorist who comes here, not just to preach, but also to bomb. The more vulnerable young in our nation, if the preachers of terrorism succeed in their rhetoric, can be enlisted to join the "cause." Congress continues to insist that a person who "merely" preaches terrorism cannot be denied entry to the US. We should do what we can to change their minds on this subject. Where do congressmen drink their coffee?

This laxity is a relatively new idea. Maintaining our borders and our choice of who enters this country is our government's solemn obligation. The Founding Fathers insisted that only those who adopted American ideals and republican principles should be allowed entry. But, this was later renounced on the grounds that it was a Cold War relic. We need to call on our leaders to revert back to the Founders' wisdom. Concern for the possible negative results to America of ideological beliefs by the illegal immigration flood is spreading across the nation. Is America in danger because of the virtual elimination of ideology as a basis for excluding foreigners? Common sense would dictate that if a foreigner is preaching the overthrow of our government and/or our system of government, he or she should not be given citizenship in our nation, or even visitation rights. Freedom of speech is one thing; freedom to call for the overthrow of our government is another thing. It is time to stop being so 'picky' about the "rights" of foreigners who preach our destruction. And, once a person becomes an American citizen, the First Amendment to the Constitution guarantees us that we join all other Americans in their rights to freedom of religion, speech, and the press, along with life, liberty and the pursuit of happiness. Yes, we have the right to access public parks, but not the right to blow them up. We have the right to attend public gatherings on the Fourth of July, but not to strap a bomb around our waist and blow ourselves up at a public gathering. Today's uni-bomber or multi-bomber from the

Middle East needs to be stopped before he goes into action. If an Islamofacist wishes us extreme evil, we simply do not invite him into our living room. If he manages to get into the living room, we retain the right to 'deport' him forthwith, whether or not he is carrying a living-room visa. The right to exclude and deport noncitizens is more than a right; it is an obligation of those in our government who are responsible for our safety and defense. The fact that millions of Mexicans are crossing our borders illegally is clear evidence that our government officials are not doing their duty. It may be very disappointing that our government has failed to prevent millions of people from entering our country illegally, but it is totally insane to pass laws that actually encourage them to do just that.

In 1798 Congress enacted the Alien Enemies Act and the Alien Act, authorizing the president to apprehend, restrain, secure, and remove alien enemies residing in the United States during times of hostility with their native country. The Alien Act granted the president discretionary authority to apprehend and deport aliens who might subvert the nation. These were the first federal laws aimed at safeguarding the nation against aliens, based on their ideology. A 1903 law provided for exclusion and deportation of foreigners who advocated violence against any government or legally passed law. Attention was paid to anyone engaged in writing or publishing any work that called for illegal activities. Also excluded were aliens who were members of associations involved in the circulation of such material. The first alien removed under this law was John Turner. During his second trip to the United States he was arrested and deported before he had a chance to speak in public. We need to return to a realistic, security-conscious policy instituted to protect us from possible future actions by a foreigner who is publicly known in Europe or any place else as one who advocates beliefs or actions that could endanger national security. Such a person should not be allowed to claim the right to be protected by the very authorities that are charged with protecting us from him. We need to recall, as a matter of vigilance, that the Soviet Comintern in 1936 ordered its members to do everything in their power to become citizens of the USA. We can presume that Islamic terrorist organizations have the same goal. From their perspective it would be foolish of them not to make such attempts.

Too Much Judicial Activism

The same judicial activism gave other rulings the same expansive interpretation of the First Amendment. The 1969 case of *Brandenburg v. Ohio* overturned a criminal statute under which a Ku Klux Klansman had made veiled threats against the U.S. president, Congress, and the judiciary. The Supreme Court ruled that "mere advocacy" of illegal acts instead of "inciting or producing imminent lawless action" should enjoy "constitutional" protection. Our nation is at such a terrorism-threatened crossroad that the Congress and the courts should revisit these kinds of rulings and make the necessary adjustments. We are no longer just facing an adversary that lives "over there;" we are facing an enemy that can now simply walk across our borders and live here. In 1987, a federal court in California ruled that Palestinian terrorist group members residing in the United States could not be deported. We are a nation that is willing to take great risks. Given the nature of Islamic terrorism, that risk-taking must stop. Let the president and our Congress in the year 2007-2008 listen to the wishes of the American people that easy access to America must be stopped. Already, many Islamic terrorist networks have taken advantage of many of the immigration loopholes, mixing with the American population by use of student and religious visas. Mosques in this nation have become hotbeds of anti-American sentiment and training schools for budding terrorists. (See my book: *Defeating Islamic Terrorism: The Wahhabi Factor.*)

Lax immigration rules allowed Ghazi Ibrahim abu Mezer to come to the United States in 1997 with the intention of bombing the New York City subway. Incredibly, he had been caught three times in one year for illegally entering the United States from Canada. When arrested, abu Mezer was out on bail during deportation proceedings, and even had the temerity to apply for political asylum. Our immigration policies and our pursuit of those who violate them are a joke. Even Hamas, the Palestinian terrorist group, ran a basic terrorist training camp outside Chicago for twenty-five Palestinians. The courses included such innocent, non-threatening subjects as car bombing! They were training in the United States to destroy, among other targets, the United States. More such meetings took place, as at Islamic conventions in Kansas City. The Palestinian Islamic Jihad also operates freely in the United States, courtesy of our immigration laws. Other terrorist notables include Dr. Yusef al-Qaradawi, homicide/suicide advocate, and Dr. Sami al-Arian, an indicted University of Florida professor. They have been welcomed to the U.S. under our lax immigration laws. And, we cannot hide even our convicted criminals, behind bars from Islamic terrorist influences, as more and more radical Islamists become chaplains in our prison system. Ideological exclusion and deportation provisions of our immigration code need to be toughened, and toughened quickly before we taste a bit of holocaust ourselves.

Let us use the First Amendment to broaden our understanding of the great gift of freedom handed down to us by Jefferson and his colleagues, not use it to destroy the freedom handed down to us by Jefferson and his colleagues. The wise Richard Malcolm Weaver, Jr (March 3, 1910 – April 1, 1963), an American scholar who taught English at the University of Chicago, left us the equally wise adage: "Ideas have consequences."

Government Neglecting Its Duty

The United States has a legitimate right, indeed a duty, to exclude from its borders foreigners whose main purpose is propagandize subjects that are inimical to the interests of the United States or could possibly undermine U.S. policy. We should restore new, strong ideological exclusion grounds to our laws. If we are going to err in the matter of immigration policy, let us err on the side of keeping Americans safe. The January 31, 1992 Summit Declaration of the United Nations Security Council agreed that threats to international peace and security can also include instability in the economic and social order, including the environment. This expanded version of national security would, therefore, most certainly include illegal immigration. So, in the age of terrorism, self-defense not only could, but should include the option of using military force, especially at our borders, but also within the inner cities of the United States that are plagued by illegal criminal gangs. They are a large and heavily armed group illegally living within our borders. They are a present danger to the United States and should be confronted by our military. The police forces in America know who they are and where they are. What are we waiting for? They constitute a direct threat, because any threat to the citizens of an American city by foreigners is a threat to the United States.

Time to Use Deadly Force

It is time to consider the use of deadly force to root out the massive buildup of illegal criminals. A gun in the hand of a foreigner is a threat. Guns in the hands of a hundred thousand foreigners living in our inner cities need to be considered very seriously and resolved by use, not only of the local and state police, but by military force. A further, though indirect, threat to national security is the threat of financial insolvency. The enormous cost of services to illegal immigrants as borne by American citizens does pose such a threat. Some argue that the United States has gained greatly from the contributions made to this nation by foreigners fleeing persecution or simply seeking a better life here. Yes, of course the United States gained from their presence, but relative to illegal immigration, this argument is specious since anyone living and working in this nation should be here legally. Our lack of enforcing our law makes a mockery of our law, and such a mockery does not engender respect for the United States. We should not mix apples and oranges when we are talking about immigrants.

Mexican/Guatemalan Border

Arriving from many other parts of the world to use the Mexico/Guatemala nexus as a jumping off point, Middle Eastern, African, and Asian aliens are among the many potential illegal threats to our national security. The Mexican-Guatemalan border is a sieve containing innumerable crossing points. The callousness of the Mexican authorities actually encouraging the violation of our borders is a slap in our face; its teamwork with Guatemalan authorities goes beyond the pale. Among any other two nations this would be tantamount to a declaration of war, with severe warnings of dire consequences being issued. The world looks on with wry humor at the manner in which Mexican authorities have interfered with our rule of law, without hesitation and without opposition by our leadership. We are the laughing stock of the world

Driver's Licenses

The 9/11 Commission recommended that drivers' licenses not be given to illegal immigrants. The mere suggestion that illegals should be issued driver licenses raised such a furor in 2007, that it greatly embarrassed the governor of New York and threatened the presidential candidacy of Hillary Clinton. It is interesting to observe, as historians have observed for hundred of years, how out of touch a nation's elite can be from the thinking of the people who elect them to office. In a democracy, such inattentiveness costs incumbents their political livelihood. What constantly amazes me is the lack of political savy on the part of politicians in the national dialogue taking place on this and similar issues. To the guy at the grocery store, or plowing the ground on his farm or fixing my car, this is a no-brainer. These good folks raise their eyebrows and ask: "Why is the granting of drivers licenses to illegals even up for discussion?" In Congress, where America's elite meet to vote it does not seem to occur to Congressmen that drivers licenses can be used to "prove" the bearers are in the country legally. Law-abiding Americans wonder why our elected representatives do not get it!! They are further shocked and dismayed when they go to Church on Saturday or Sunday and their minister agrees with the Congress. It's an eerie feeling that no one in authority has any common sense. The December 1, 2004 edition of the Washington Times quoted Joan Molinaro, mother of a New York City firefighter who died in the Twin Tower disaster. "You allowed the murder of my son. I will not allow you to kill my daughters...No bill should pass the Senate, the House, anywhere, unless you secure our borders-you keep my girls alive."

Deport Radical Islamists Immediately

The need to pay attention to Ms. Molinaro is clear when we recall the bombing of the World Trade Center by Middle East immigrant terrorists and the murder of CIA agents in the fall of 1992. The link between immigration and terrorism is now too obvious to ignore. This obvious link sparked passage of both the Violent Crime Control and Law Enforcement Act of 1994 and the Antiterrorism and Effective Death Penalty Act of 1996. It also brought forth Republican and Democratic unity, as exemplified by the cooperation between Lamar Smith (R-TX), and Edward M. Kennedy (D-MA), who took similar positions on the need to be aware of the dangers right here at home from illegal aliens. Smith was forthright in saying: "Our immigration laws and procedures are being overwhelmed by applicants for asylum, many of whom are making fraudulent claims, and some of whom are terrorists." Kennedy said, "A clear sign of the crisis in illegal immigration is that we have lost control over the process for removing illegal and especially, illegal criminals from the United States"

How is it, for example, that radical Islamic preacher Sheik Omar Abdel Rahman was able to enter this nation, even though he was on the Department of

State's watch list as a security threat? The threat from radical Islam can be demonstrated in the example of Rahman, a blind sheik who is currently in prison in the United States because of his role in bomb plots in New York City. What most people do not know about him, however, is that he is considered an Islamic spiritual leader and role model by Osama bin Laden and his top lieutenants. Sheik Omar Abdel Rahman's involvement with terrorism was nothing new to authorities. His name came to the surface when he was involved in the plot to assassinate Egyptian president Anwar Sadat, and when he was known to be the spiritual leader of a radical group called Jama'at al-Jihad. He was not shy about making his views publicly known. In answer to the question: What would you do to a ruler who has ignored the law of God? -a question asked of him a year before Sadat was assassinated, he replied: "Death." Rahman was indicted for participating in the issuance of a fatwa ordering Sadat's murder. He was acquitted, but he hardly lay low. On October 1st, 1995, Rahman was convicted with nine others for their involvement in a conspiracy to plant bombs at New York landmarks like the United Nations building and FBI offices. If the connection between terrorism and illegal immigration stopped there, it would have been bad enough. Recall that three of the nineteen September 11 terrorists were in the country illegally, having overstayed the time allowed them in the country. Seven of the nineteen highjackers carried fake ID cards. More than 100,000 people from Middle Eastern countries reside in the

United States illegally, some of them through the courtesy of convicted criminal George Tajirian.

George Tajirian

The Iraqi, George Tajirian, who forged an alliance with a Mexican immigration officer, Angel Molina Paramo, smuggled Palestinian, Jordanian, Syrian, Iraqi, Yemeni and other undocumented immigrants through Mexico into the United States, where Mr. Molina was based as an immigration officer until his arrest in 1999. He also helped the clients make contact with local smugglers in northern Mexico. Of course they did not come empty-handed. They carried with them travel documents from, among other places, Greece and Mexico. Paramo was an equal opportunity smuggler, not favoring any particular political or revolutionary agenda. They focused on the Southwestern states. Through that portal they delivered hundreds of Middle Eastern illegals into the United State. Mr. Tajirian's wife, a Mexican, was also accused, along with a Lebanese woman who ran Mr. Tajirian's travel agency in Quito, Ecuador. The prosecutors estimated that he led more than one thousand Middle East natives across the southwest frontier, lost in a sea of Hispanics. That ride across wind-driven sand cost his clients $10,000 to $15,000 each. Middle Easterners also like to enter the United States via the Canadian border. How many of them have terrorist backgrounds? How many of them have taken up positions as sleeper contacts for future bombing missions in this country? We have no idea. What we do know is that terrorists can exploit our weak immigration policies, and that porous borders and such policies can no longer be tolerated in the age of modern and highly effective terrorism.

Monitoring Foreign Students

There are more than 600,000 foreign students studying at American universities. The FBI has concerns about many of them, and has warned Congress that state sponsors of terrorism are sponsoring scholarships for students to come to the U.S. and enroll in high-tech-related studies that could contribute to the development of powerful military ordnance. A computerized system to track foreign students, the Coordinated Interagency Partnership Regarding International Students, or CIPRIS, was never put in place. After September 11, Congress required an automated system to maintain information on foreign students, and one was developed. It is called, The Student and Exchange Visitor Information System (SEVIS). It is capable of tracking immigration status changes, changes of address, and changes in program of study. DHS action on information provided is needed for the information to succeed in detecting any potentially dangerous student.

No-Brainer

With twelve to twenty million illegal aliens living in the United States and nearly one million new aliens arriving each year, the potential for terrorists entering the United States undetected is very high. If a terrorist wants to enter the United States, all he has to do is take a Sunday afternoon stroll across the

Mexican border. Our government is still looking for the 300,000-plus foreigners, whose names are known by the FBI, who have disappeared. This came to light only when it was determined that they should be deported. We open our borders to illegal aliens; we then judge that they must leave our country; they then disappear in our country and we cannot find them. There is something radically wrong with this scenario. Our government should take a good look at all visa applications from young men from Muslim countries. It has been eight years since 9/11, and it took our government several years to come to a sensible conclusion: that since nineteen young men from Muslim countries were involved in the 9/11 disaster, we should now start taking a closer look at young Muslims asking to enter the United States. Better late than never, but still quite late. And yet, some refuse to see a connection between terrorism prevention and immigration policy. Cecilia Munoz of the National Council of La Raza believes "There's no relationship between immigration and terrorism." Jeanne Butterfield, executive director of the American Immigration Lawyers Association echoed this same 'brilliant' conclusion. "I don't think the events of last week (9/11) can be attributed to the failure of our immigration laws." I am all for replacing all educated folks in important jobs with farmers. Common sense is incredibly lacking in corporate and governmental offices. But I would be happy to make an exception in the case of Steven Camarota, Center for Immigration Studies. Here is what he said: "Because every part of our immigration system has been exploited by terrorists, we cannot reform just one area, but must address the problems that exist throughout. The solution is not to single out Middle Easterners for exclusion or selective enforcement. Instead we need to more carefully check the backgrounds of all visa applicants, better police the borders, strictly enforce the law within the country, and, most importantly, reduce the level of immigration to give government agencies the breathing space necessary to implement fundamental reforms." Amen to that.

Chapter Ten

The Balkanization of America

Invasion, Not Evolution

We are moving into a new world, a world more reminiscent of historical and, in Europe, recent examples of balkanization, as the face of America changes. "Balkanization" is the temporary or permanent division of a nation along the lines of ethnic or religious differences. This has not been a problem for the United States, but since it is now becoming a reality, it should be addressed. In America, the problem is not one of ethnicity or race for, as we have noted, America has evolved in accordance with its unique role as an immigrant nation. The problem is that if unbridled illegal immigration continues, then the dominant group would not represent the thinking and the evolutionary development of the nation; rather, it will reflect the thinking of aliens who occupied us illegally. It would be change by invasion, not evolution. Let us take an example. If illegals from Continental Europe flooded into England and the illegals outpaced the English in numbers, the illegals would then take over England. That, obviously, would be wrong. Yet, this is what will happen soon in the United States if there is no change in immigration policy. And, it is simply amazing to watch it all happening, led by recent presidents of the United States, the ones charged by the Constitution to see that such illegal entry not take place. They have been contributing to, not opposing, the illegal invasion of the United States. At a minimum, that constitutes a dereliction of duty. I leave it to the legal scholars to say whether we now have a president who is also brazenly flouting the law and getting away with it because the Congress is belly gazing rather than doing its job. Unfortunately, America is too preoccupied with Madonna and other Hollywood stars to take notice.

The Coming Demise of the Multi-Cultural Society

One of great prides of living in America has been that we live harmoniously in a multicultural society. However, massive illegal immigration and a resurgence of 'nationalism' among us have reached a level that is beginning to cause collective anxiety. The pride of the diversity of multiculturalism is now devolving into the fear of multicultural racial and ethnic antagonism, making the likelihood of preserving, even salvaging, national unity a pipe dream. Can cultural diversity overpower unity-in-diversity? Yes, it certainly can. We need not dig into ancient history to find an example of what might await us. The splintering of Lebanon and former Yugoslavia are present-day examples. Is our nation so unique that we can escape the fate of Yugoslavia? If, as the U.S. Bureau of the Census estimates, we will be a nation of 420 million by the year 2050 and, given the present rate of illegal immigration, what will that mean in terms of who we will be as a nation? Well, for one thing, the nation will be divided into different blocs, with perhaps no clear majority among them. It could happen that Americans of European origin will be in the minority. Once again, what I would like to emphasize is that if this happened naturally, no problem. Power centers shift all the time. It is a natural evolution of history. But, if it is happening to us without our consent and at the direction of the same president that we elected to protect our borders, this is a very serious situation, a national disaster. Only an enlightened church leadership would have the moral authority to alert the nation.

Considering that the European-origin population founded and directed the development of the United States, and did a very good job at it, what will a different ethnic or racial equality or even majority mean for America's culture? Culture determines an approach to foreign policy, economics, the choice of legal systems, the inter-relationships of co-workers, the relationships between married couples, etc. To allow an illegal invasion of foreigners, no matter how nice they are, is to kill the nation, to self-destruct. Such a configuration of America, if that is what happens, would suggest that the United States of 2050 may be a balkanized America with no common unity, with no thread to hold it together, an America that has lost its present soul. The suggestion of many scholars that it will be "an America without Americans" is not all that far-fetched.

Ethnicity may well determine the centers of power. And that is fine, if it is a natural historical evolution. But, what is happening in America is not natural. It is an invasion. It is an invasion aided and abetted by corrupt politicians avidly seeking voters, American or not. It is an invasion aided and abetted by greedy capitalists, an invasion that has the uninformed blessings of the Christian church.

Shift to the Left

As has already been noticed by political and media observers, the nation will begin to steer itself to the left of the political spectrum, for the poor will become the majority in power; the poor are always liberal because they have nothing to lose. One can see in the 2008 electoral campaign a subtle appeal, even by Republicans, to the massive wave of Hispanic immigration. The so-called powerless are becoming powerful. Three cheers for them, I say, but only if they are doing it within the boundaries and laws of our nation.

Transitional Period

While there is little doubt that the three major groupings will be able to sustain a modicum of unity during a transition stage, it is almost inevitable that this will not last, especially since two of the groups are non-white and have been, historically, not part of the in-crowd. At some point, blacks will want to declare their long-sought independence. It would, initially, be a further step in a process of complete liberation that began with freedom from slavery. At some point in time, however, it is historically inevitable that politically correct American unity will fray at the edges. It will lead eventually to de facto balkanization. While on the one hand, there is a certain moderate tension between Hispanics and blacks relative to a larger piece of the American pie, eventually that moderate tension may develop into keen competition. There has been, in our nation, a certain natural alliance between the black and Hispanic communities relative to the white community. However, in the future configuration it is likely that that unity, already fragile because illegal immigrants are now taking jobs away from black youth, will break out into a certain competitiveness that could get ugly. That will depend on how skillfully that relationship is handled. While all of this is going on, mass immigration will further bring various pots to boil. One could envision a determined effort by the black community to recruit blacks from Africa and the Caribbean, to keep up with the pace of Hispanic presence. In this case, the present ideal of ethnic and racial assimilation will shatter and, in one sense at least, the black community will go back to ethnic isolation, but this time on an equal basis. The American dream of one people under God with liberty and justice for all, the dream that the black community has died and prayed for since slavery, may no longer be anyone's ideal. When that happens, then the three groups will move in entirely different directions. Explicit racial and ethnic consciousness will then become king. It is at that point that the balkanization of America will take place. And then the labels of Republican and Democrat will cease to have any meaning. No longer would the party system be viable. The gradual entrenchment of balkanization will make the old political labels irrelevant. It will then be the European bloc, the African-American bloc and the Spanish bloc. Each block will be relentlessly political. There will be a new founding of America that will demand the balkanization of America, an inevitable event that then will make the term "American" lose its traditional meaning. "America" will then refer, not to a Jeffersonian ideal, but a physical location somewhere in a 'three-nation' America. When one considers that there is already close to a one-million-a-year increase in the Hispanic population alone, the move to bring in more blacks to balance that out will not only be intense, but will also likely fail, for the Hispanic population is already larger, and their copatriots can just walk across our border. .

In the short term, Hispanic interests will increasingly determine American foreign policy. Balkanization is already taking place in Los Angeles and Miami. Even Tyson Foods creates Hispanic enclaves wherever it settles. They are very fond of employing Mexicans as cheap labor, an insult to Hispanics. It is the business community that is driving the balkanization of America. It is not doing so consciously; it is doing it, in fact, blindly, blinded by greed. It feeds its ravenous engines with illegal labor. Illegal labor becomes, in one way or another, part of the American landscape. As part of the American landscape it does two things: (a) it grows in numbers and (b), once it grows in numbers it grows in political and economic influence. So, the engine driving balkanization is business.

Ironically, while American troops are courageously fighting against enormous odds in Afghanistan and Iraq, the shortage of troops along our borders is giving away the nation. Maybe it was inevitable. Maybe we deserve it because we failed to see what was going on. I cannot say, but I can say that it is happening. The Wall Street Journal has even editorialized in favor of open borders. Simple common sense tells us that we cannot expect to switch populations through massive immigration and not expect, also, to switch the civilizations and symbols that represent them. You cannot expect millions of aliens from one culture to enter the country, abandon all loyalties and values of their old civilization, and assimilate the new one, most especially if they are the majority.

The Evolution of Ethnic Leadership

Americans of European origin will be leaderless at the beginning of balkanization. They will need to develop leadership, the kind of leadership represented in the black community by Al Sharpton and Jesse Jackson. It is not surprising that they do not have that leadership because they were, as an entity, the leadership of this nation. Now that balkanization is their future, only a European leadership that holds the European-American community together will save it from losing its way in the new world. African-Americans have been, unconsciously, building this leadership ever since slavery. It is vital, it is strong and it has been essential to their survival. The balkanization of America is going to take place in spite of the determination on the part of an American president, a Mexican president and the Canadian prime minister to develop a strong North American Union. Such a Union can only evolve if the ethnicity is relational. The Germans, the English, the Italians and the French, together with the Scandinavian immigrants, do see themselves cut from the same continental cloth. In our case, the Hispanic and African-American communities will not feel that relational bond. Globalization is a pipe dream. Communism proved it. It behooves the European-American community to study the history and politics of the balkanization of Eastern Europe.

The Wild Card

In almost every complicated matter of importance in our lives, there is the presence of the wild card, the card that can change the entire game plan. In our case, the wild card can either extend the life of the coming tripartite leadership in America, or hasten the arrival of American balkanization. The wild card is the present Mexican-American (legal) population. To tip the balancing act of the coming tripartite leadership, the Mexican-American leadership is needed. Up until 2007, they appeared to have little interest in playing the Hispanic card. They had not shown any more intense interest than other ethnic groups in 'flaunting' their ethnic background or running to the defense of their governments of origin. If we were making a judgment prior to 2007, our judgment probably would have been that they would not radically swing in favor of more power on the American scene. We might also have made the judgment that Hispanic Americans, over time, exhibited the same diminution of group ethnic identity as any other ethnic immigrant group. Now, all bets are off. The homogenization of differences among people of Latin American origin in the United States is part of the process of racialization. For many people of Latin American origin, their common experience of life in the United States, rather than different national Hispanic origins, is the foundation for melding their common interests. Unlike the Africans who arrived in America in chains, most persons of Latin American origin came to the United States believing in the American Dream.

Chapter Eleven

Thoughts on Globalization

David Rockefeller has written in his book Memoirs, "Some believe we (the Rockefeller family) are part of a secret cabal working against the best interests of the United States, and of conspiring with others around the world to build a more integrated global political and economic structure---one world, if you will. If that's the charge, I stand guilty, and I am proud of it."

A friend of David Rockefeller wrote: "David has supported a multidimensional strategy comprising US global leadership, the United Nations, multinational corporations, international economic integration, global and regional free trade, and global governance."

"In the next century, nations as we know [them] will be obsolete; all states will recognize a single, global authority. National sovereignty wasn't such a great idea after all". – Strobe Talbot, President Clinton's deputy secretary of state, as quoted in Time,

July 20, 1992

Richard Haass, the current president of the Council on Foreign Relations, stated in his article "State sovereignty must be altered in globalized era," that a system of world government must be created and sovereignty eliminated in order to fight global warming, as well as terrorism."Moreover, states must be prepared to cede some sovereignty to world bodies if the international system is to function," says Haass. "Globalization thus implies that sovereignty is not only becoming weaker in reality, but that it needs to become weaker."

In March 2005 at their summit meeting in Waco, Texas, President Bush, Mexico's President Fox and Canada's Prime Minister Martin issued a joint statement announcing the creation of the "Security and Prosperity Partnership of North America" (SPP). Short circuiting the Congress, the U.S. Department of Commerce merely created a new division under the same title to implement working groups to advance a North American Union working agenda that included: manufactured goods, movement of goods, energy, environment, e-commerce, financial services, business facilitation, food and agriculture, transportation, and health. SPP is headed by three top cabinet level officers of each country. Representing the United States in 2008 were the secretary of commerce, the secretary of homeland security, and secretary of state.

Working groups were established to make recommendations to the heads of state, without any reference to congressional oversight. This is stated in the report to the heads of state. "This is not a theoretical exercise being prepared so it can be submitted for review." Instead, SPP is producing an action agreement to be implemented directly by regulations, without any envisioned direct Congressional oversight. "Upon your review and approval, we will once again meet with stakeholders and work with them to implement the work plans that we have developed."

The work plans submitted by the working groups use language such as "our three countries signed a Framework of Common Principles..." or "we have signed a Memorandum of Understanding ...," or "we have signed a declaration of intent..." etc. There is no mention in the thirty or more working agendas of any communication with or approval by the U.S. Congress. All of this is taking place under the political or judicial radar. It is being done by presidential fiat. We now have an answer to the question of why our borders are not secure. The answer is that in all the reports to the heads of state there is an emphasis on free and open movement of people, trade, and capital within the North American Union. Once the SPP agenda is implemented, immigration policy, trade rules, environmental regulations, and other important decisions will be decided not by the United States Congress, but by the heads of state of the three nations, upon advice from the SPP working groups. There will be no "border" with Mexico to discuss or protect. On the Mexican website, ASPAN, the SPP is described as "a permanent, tri-lateral process to create a major integration of North America." Significantly, the working group activity follows a blueprint announced in the May 2005 report of the Council on Foreign Relations (CFR), titled "Building a North American Community." The SPP working groups' recommendation is that by 2010, the only borders or tariffs that would remain would be those circumscribing the continent, not those between the three nations. What will happen to the sovereignty of the United States? The template is the European Community. A central authority will be created that will serve the interests of the SPP, a parliamentary body that will not replace so much as supersede the individual nations' courts. The U.S. dollar will be replaced by a common currency, named for the moment the "Amero."

The Negative Effects Of Globalization

Anyone who is having trouble with his or her Cable TV and calls for help may chat with a young man or woman from India. That same household may have one or more members looking for work. United States corporations neglect their countrymen by outsourcing manufacturing and white-collar jobs. Other types of jobs are outsourced to China where the cost of manufacturing goods and wages are lower, and the job does not require the speaking of English. Even highly educated American scientists have a tenuous hold on some jobs because of outsourcing. McDonalds, KFC and other service industries are spreading like wildfire in the developing world. The rich are getting richer and the poor are becoming poorer, as customer services, marketing and software development join the ranks of the outsourced.

A very fancy name is given to the movement of factories that should be employing Americans relocating to the Third and Fourth worlds. The factory owners say they are moving to free trade zones. Sounds nice but it is an expression that covers up the exploitation and the oppression of working men and women all around the globe to feed the bulging coffers of greedy business executives. Moving to a free trade zone located in a poor nation is the equivalent of conquering that poor nation without firing a shot. It is the domination of European and American capital over domestic capital and even to some extent political power over that poor state. It is estimated that there are more than 750,000 Mexican factory employees working in jobs Americans would have today, if they had not been taken south.

NAFTA Is Globalization Fast Forward

The opening salvo for the creation of a North American Union was the creation of NAFTA. The backers of NAFTA are in a hurry. In its report, *Building a North American Community,* the Council on Foreign Relations is for the "creation by 2010 of a North American Community...Its boundaries will be defined by a common external tariff and an outer security perimeter within which the movement of people, products, and capital will be legal, orderly, and safe."

The plan was strongly supported by President Bush who publicly announced on February 16,

2001, that the United States, Canada and Mexico, "will strive to consolidate a North American economic community. " NAFTA is the foundation stone for such a North American Union. Clinton and his predecessor, George Bush senior, who attended the signing of the North American Free Trade Agreement on September 14, 1993, assured the American people that NAFTA would increase American employment and be a shot in the arm to the economy. In fact, according to the Economic Policy Institute, by 2006, NAFTA had cost the United States a million jobs. Some estimates are much higher. In any case, what NAFTA has really put in motion is an ongoing process of influencing our national, state and local governments to new regional institutions. Referring to the present administration, Lou Dobbs, in a June 21, 2007 broadcast, said this: "The Bush administration's decision to back an open-borders policy and its decision to ignore the enforcement of this country's immigration laws is part of a broader agenda. " Lou Dobbs then states that in setting up the Security and Prosperity Partnership (SPP), the President "will end the United States as we know it."

Henry Kissinger has been an open admirer of NAFTA. He wrote in the Los Angeles Times that the approval of NAFTA could go down in history as the most important act taken by the Clinton Congress. The passage of NAFTA he said "will represent the most creative step toward a new world order taken by any group of countries since the end of the Cold

War, the first step toward an even larger vision of a free-trade zone for the entire Western Hemisphere."

The reality is that NAFTA is the chicken that will lay the egg of the continental common market. This is clear when you consider that the agreement assumes the establishment of extraterritorial trade panels to decide on labor and environmental disputes. In a November 13, 1993 radio address, President Clinton openly said, contradicting his own defenders: "This is not a Trade Summit. It is an *overall* Summit." His Chief of Staff Mack McLarty said: "It will focus on economic integration and convergence."

The NAFTA Reality

The continuing, unabated, invasion of illegals either from Mexico or through Mexico proves free trade has been a clear and objective failure. The United States moved more than 4,000 factories to Mexico in order to make more money for the factory owners and "to save the Mexican economy." It certainly did make more money for factory owners but did not benefit poor Mexicans. If it had, there would be less illegal immigration, not more. So, since the much-heralded NAFTA was passed, conditions got so bad in Mexico that the United States had to pour billions of dollars into Mexico to stabilize the peso. Mexico's agricultural industry has been devastated. Heavily subsidized American farmers have taken over the agricultural market simply because the Mexican government either is unable or unwilling to match the subsidy the Americans receive. Rosario Nobles, leader of a Mexican opposition party said:

"The countryside is a time-bomb that could explode very soon." The farmers are the most vocal opposition group opposing NAFTA. NAFTA contributed to further impoverishing Mexico and the United States. It proved to be a Trojan horse that contained an army of armed economic "special forces" assigned to destroy the respective economies. NAFTA set the rules for a race to the economic bottom. Franklin Delano Roosevelt said economic diseases are highly communicable. With Church leaders innocently (for lack of understanding of the issues involved) advocating the continued presence of illegals among us, we are in for quite an economic pandemic. Immigration lawyers, however, are having a great time. They are reported to be hale, hearty and, we might add, wealthy.

Why Does Third World Court NAFTA?

Now, if NAFTA has been such a disaster for the ordinary Third World laborer, why is it that Third World nations continue to seek the establishment of American and European factories on their soil? The answer may surprise you. As a former advisor to a Third World government, I can give you a bit of insight. Corporations claim (correctly) that the governments of Third World countries want them to invest in their nations, but what does that really mean? There is one scenario that can explain why some Third World leaders, although they know what is happening in Mexico, still seek the presence of large corporations on their soil. These governments are under such pressure to increase exports before they can benefit from IMF financial help that they will accept the 'book' appearance of exports that foreign factories are producing. Of course, except for a modicum amount of low-wage jobs, the foreign factory presence does little for the local economy. The profits are exported. That fact, plus the possibility of personally benefiting from corporation bribes usually wins the day. Do the leaders know that what they are doing will further weaken their economies? Generally speaking they do know, but retaining their jobs and luxurious lifestyles is their chief concern. The problem before these leaders is that they must make hay while the sun shines, because they know very well that if the foreign companies find a better deal anywhere, they will cut and run. A local employer would keep the profits within the country, resulting in an improvement in the physical and social infrastructure, but the World Community is blindly ignoring this obvious fact. We could all help the Third World by such a program, but no one seems to want to take the initiative of getting the process started.

Before I Close

Let me share with you an exchange of mail I had with a few Mexican women on their feelings about the growth of illegal immigration into the United States. Their words might surprise you. The first woman to write to me wishes to remain anonymous for fear of retaliation. She works with the abandoned wives and children of men who are working illegally in the United States. Her mail was a response to an mail I sent after being informed that a group of Mexican women had decided that, with their husbands having left for the United States to find work, some of who now had begun new families, the women had to find a way to support themselves and their children.

Her first reply to my mail:

> "Dear Father Bascio I was given your article by women of -----. It is very interesting and agreeable - p.s. yes, your main thesis is most powerfully demonstrated. What is it you are looking for from them? How can we help you? *Saludos amigo*"

Her second email described her work and the heartbreaking lives of women abandoned by their husbands to live in America.

> "I live in ---- and --- since the early 1970s working with a rural women's artisan cooperative for past ten of fifteen years, but not in the capacity of an aid worker or anything like that. I am just another campesina girl on my best days mopping the shop floor. Still, I am providing technical support for the jewelry production operation run by these women. Actually I am in the process of writing a book that we intend to self-publish in the next weeks. It is a project book of how to make your own traditional Mexican jewelry. This book of ours includes some letters from the women that I translated into English - But, you don't really need that raw material, do you padre? I think maybe all you need is to interview me because I know dozens of persons who are illegal Mexicans in the USA. More than half the men of Tecalpulco are

in the USA today. My in-laws are all in Chicago cleaning bowling alleys and gymnasiums, and I have friends in Phoenix, New Jersey, Los Angeles. I am working every day in the jewelry shop with the women who are the unrecognized other half of the illegal alien - when these women hear that Mexicans are to be offered citizenship in the United States - HOW do you think that makes them feel? The men only had permission to go up there for a little while to get some money and come back and improve the house. They never had permission to make another family over there and then go apply for citizenship. Lots of other crazy stuff like all the murderers automatically goes over there, so the United States is sowing the seeds of its destruction when it destroys families and wrecks traditional life..."

I also received this communication:

"*Tecalpulco*, Municipio de Taxco de Alarcon, Guerrero, México

From the women and children of Mexico, to the people of the USA -

Enforce your laws.

Please close the United States border to illegal migration.

Help us to keep our husbands home with our families.

(Only, please, treat our brothers and husbands in a humane manner –

Please do not hurt them) "

Letters to husbands from village women in Guerrero, Mexico. Your heart will go out to these women and to the millions like them who live in the Third and Fourth Worlds.

"Dear Pedro, how I miss you. You said you were only going to Arizona to get money for our house but now you have been away and did not come back when your sister got married. Oh how I worry that you have another woman! Don't you love me? You told me you love me. You love me. I know you love me and our life together..."

"Dear Ruben, please come home the children have not seen you in three years and little Beto is a young man and Lupita asks about her papa. I know we agreed you should try your fortune in the United States, but I didn't know that it would be so lonely and that you would be gone for such a long time. Please return to us."

"Dearest Luis,

When you called on the telephone I was so happy to hear your voice and to know that you had passed safely over to the other side of the border. Good luck. God will help you. Your mother is here with me I will take care of her until you return. Work hard; don't drink, save money and come back to the children and me. "

Another.

"...because you don't want to believe that I love you....Even though always you say the opposite....I will be, all my life, the love that remained sunken in its pain because you did not want to love....,"

Taxco, Gro. Mex, the 15th of November of

2007

Another

"(Father Pat) you can attribute the letter from the sister, Lorena, to her brother. She is a young woman from Huematla, Guerrero, Mexico.

For Arturo

"Hello brother I hope you find yourself well. I know I have not written you since the last two times I wrote you since you went and will not be able to forget that day that I was the last person you saw and to whom you said goodbye that goodbye was as if we were going to see each other the next day, so we wouldn't feel that nostalgia that is felt when a loved one goes and it is when one appreciates that person. I know that when you left the house papa and mama were very sad, especially mama, since she was crying and crying, even though for some days she was calm but only heard her name or said words that you always said or things they remembered of you and they started to cry inconsolably, apart from what you would already know before you left occurred the death of grandmother Angela, in all they were days of sadness and nostalgia for all of us, the death of a family member, and your leaving.

"We put up with the passing of the days, weeks, and months we are overcoming, thus we are more tranquil with respect to those bad times and we remember better the moments we passed happily together and still of course almost always with you, almost always Emma, Erica, and me, we who are your sisters. We had a different form of thinking, and in opinion of something, as opposed to you who usually always would take contrarily, for which we always fought but already it does not make sense for me to talk of that to you because even though we had our differences, I know we love each other very much. And that we miss you hoping for your soon return home even though I already know that you are not going to return for a long time, since for you it was very difficult to pass the frontier of the United States, for the difficult moments that you went through for having walked days through the desert suffering from much heat that burnt your feet and at night enduring cold that just about froze you, for which I know very well that you will not return soon, for all that you suffered and endured.

"I hope that these negative moments convert themselves for you in positive moments and in realized dreams thus it is that I desire for you all the luck in the world so that your dreams are realized and hoping you soon return here to your family.

"Papa and mama and we your sisters we send you greetings and embraces with much tenderness and affection desiring you the best of fortune s where you find yourself. Also I know that your birthday is nearing in this month of December don't believe that I have forgotten I have it before me the same as with papa, mama, Erica, Emma,... thus it is that at the right time I will send you a present or a detail, well now yes I say my good-bye to you, but not as if we were not going to see each other soon, this good-bye is as if we were going to see each other in a week, or in a few days, so how do you like it if I say to you that we will see each other soon and that you are well like that last day that we said good-bye to each other as if we were going to see each other later that day in the house. Well that is all. Farewell to you, your sister who has you present each day."

From: Lorena

"Father Pat: The poignant love letter was written in Tecalpulco and the fragment is from a letter written by someone in the village of Taxco El Viejo. Best wishes and Keep in touch.

"Honestly, I love you....
To again have you in my life....
To again look into your eyes....
To feel your gaze....
My heart beats again
It is to again remember
those beautiful moments together

"Many times I accept looking at you to see that you move away from me,

I wanted to run to your side, to tell you I love you, but I remained in silence,

because I knew I had lost you forever.....

"You don't know how much pain, I can't tell it to you....you don't know what it is to remain thinking that you left and if you will return, each morning waking up to have the hope that you return, life is uncertain, and as of today you haven't come back

"Always in my mind remained that day I say you depart, that you left, that you left behind a great love. Even though I try to know what is the truth of your love the years passed I never had your kisses instead of those remained your memories....my tears and the rancor of having lost you...But you should always know that I love you like no other and that never I would tell it to you because your heart was no longer mine....and that that pain is, will be mine forever...

"Now you know that in this life there exists one person who loves you, who will live loving you eternally forever....you trapped my heart, you had me in your arms, and you didn't know how to value it....

"To say I love you...Only you will hear it said by me...To say it not only is it a word It Means that all my feelings will be for ever for you....you are for me that love that I never will forget. Only God and my heart know all the love I feel for you."

Taxco de Alarcon, Guerrero, México

From: Women in Tecalpulco, Municipio de Taxco de Alarcon, Guerrero, México

"Father Pat:

"The work is in the United States that is why the men left, leaving millions of broken families in the villages. Now our men are running from the police, but we have organized our village cottage industry around the traditional handicraft jewelry of our region of Mexico. Our village of Tecalpulco was very successful in the 1980s, when our parents were the creators of the abalone shell jewelry.

"Ours is a beautiful place to live and since we have organized and begun to have some success our hope is that the Mexican men who have gone to the US return.

"We don't need anybody's help for we are proud artisans. Not anyone can make the kind of beautiful jewelry we make in our workshops. God will help us to meet the needs of our family to surmount the great difficulties we have always faced, as Mexican women over the centuries.

"WE WANT TO WORK AT WHAT WE ARE GOOD AT.

WE WANT OUR MEN WHO ARE WORKING IN THE UNITED STATES TO RETURN TO THEIR HOMES AND FAMILIES AND HELP US MAKE JEWELRY AND BE HAPPY."

-o-

INDEX

CURRICULUM VITAE

Father Patrick Bascio, C.S.Sp.

Email: pajbascio@yahoo.com

Education:

Bachelor in Philosophy, Masters in Theology, St. Mary's, Norwalk Ct,

Masters in Psychology, St. Joseph's, Mount Vernon, NY

PhD in Systematic Theology, with emphasis on Morality of Economic and Political Systems, Fordham University, Bronx, New York City

Experience:

At present: Retired as Trinidad and Tobago Province Peace and Justice Coordinator for Holy Ghost Fathers.

2000-2008: Peace and Justice Coordinator for Holy Ghost Fathers in Trinidad and Tobago

1996-2000: Pastoral work in Trinidad and sabbatical in Florida

1992-1995: Research at Harvard University: Pastor, Our Lady of Divine Providence, Providenciales, Turks and Caicos Islands, and *ad hoc* representative of UN High Commission for Refugees.

1985-1992: Director of Master's Program in Humanities and Founder and Director of PhD Program in Humanities, Salve Regina University, Newport, RI. Founder of Masters program for high ranking U.S. and Allied military at United States Naval War College, Newport, RI .

1979-1985: Pastor, St. Mark Evangelist Church, Harlem, New York City, and Economic Advisor to Grenada's Ambassador to the United Nations.

1974-1978: Member of Grenada Diplomatic Mission to the United Nations, with diplomatic rank of Counselor, and Economic Advisor to the Prime Minister. Grenada representative to 3rd and 5th UN Committees.

1962-1974: Pastor, Catholic Church, Carriacou, Grenada. Lecturer in Black Studies, University of West Indies, Port of Spain, Trinidad and pastoral work in Trinidad.

1955-1962: Ordination to priesthood; Lecturer in Physics, Umbwe College, Mt. Kilimanjaro, Tanzania

1947-1955: Studies for Priesthood at St Mary's, Norwalk, Ct.

1944-1946: U.S. Army Air Corps Pacific Theater

For Ordering Additional Copies of On The Immorality of Illegal Immigration By Father Patrick Bascio (Revised Edition)

On-Line Orders: Go to ***AuthorHouse.com***. Click on ***Bookstore*** to enter bookstore browser. Enter ***Bascio*** in the search window of the bookstore browser. When the Bascio book image appears click on ***Add to Cart***. Then click on ***Proceed to Checkout*** and provide information on number of copies needed, shipping address and method, billing information, and credit card information for payment to complete order. Address e-mail inquiries to customersupport@authorhouse.com

Telephone Orders: Dial Author House Book Sales toll free at 1-888 519-5121 Extension 5023 or 1-888 280-7715. Have ready Bascio book title and ISBN number (ISBN 9781449001858) and credit card information for customer support representative who will assist you. The general purpose toll-free number for Author House books is 1-800 839-8640

Mail Inquiries: Address all mail inquiries about book purchases with name address and phone number to:

Customer Support
Author House Books
Suite 1663 Liberty Drive, Suite 200
Bloomington, IN 47403

Book Store Purchases: *On the Immorality of Illegal Immigration,* by Father Patrick Bascio (ISBN 9781449001858), can also be ordered through major bookstores and through amazon.com.

LaVergne, TN USA
18 September 2009
158379LV00001B/2/P